CONTENTS

CRISIS IN THE GALAXY

THE DARK SIDE RISES

For over a thousand generations, Jedi Knights served the Old Republic as guardians of peace. But war loomed on the horizon as evil Sith Lord Darth Sidious set into motion the final stages of an ancient plan to destroy the Jedi Order.

66 BSI*

INVASION OF NABOO

With Darth Sidious pulling the strings from the shadows, the Trade Federation invaded the peaceful planet Naboo with its droid army. Jedi Master Qui-Gon Jinn and his apprentice, Obi-Wan Kenobi, reached the planet and rescued Queen Padmé Amidala.

ANAKIN SKYWALKER

On their way to the Galactic Senate, Qui-Gon Jinn and Obi-Wan Kenobi encountered nine-year-old Anakin Skywalker on the planet Tatooine. The Force was exceptionally strong with the boy, and Qui-Gon decided to take Anakin to the Jedi Temple on Coruscant.

BATTLE OF NAB

On Naboo, the Trade army was defeated. Duri Gon Jinn and Obi-Wan fierce Sith warrior Dart Lord eventually fell, b fatally injured.

* When Starkiller Base destroyed the Hosnian System is taken as year 0 in the Age of Resistance.
All events are marked by years BSI (Before Starkiller Incident) and ASI (After Starkiller Incident)

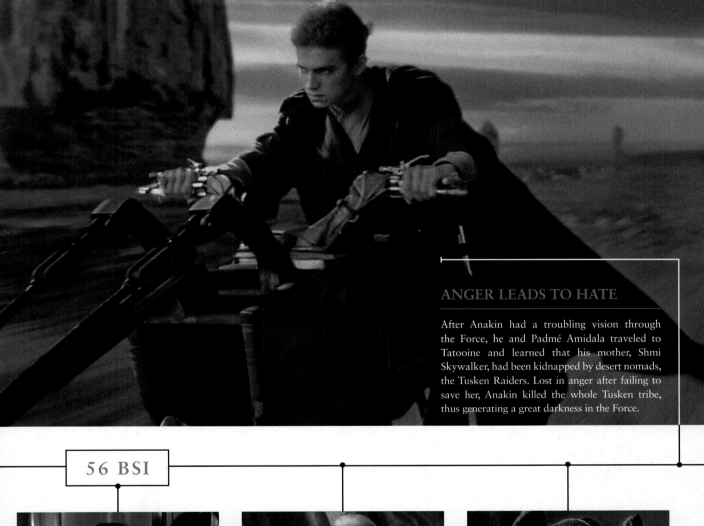

ANGER LEADS TO HATE

After Anakin had a troubling vision through the Force, he and Padmé Amidala traveled to Tatooine and learned that his mother, Shmi Skywalker, had been kidnapped by desert nomads, the Tusken Raiders. Lost in anger after failing to save her, Anakin killed the whole Tusken tribe, thus generating a great darkness in the Force.

56 BSI

A NEW APPRENTICE

Despite concerns from the 12 members of the Jedi High Council, who had sensed a strong presence of fear in Anakin Skywalker when they had met him, Obi-Wan Kenobi had decided to follow Qui-Gon Jinn's last will and for the last ten years had been training Anakin as his own apprentice.

THE SEPARATISTS

Thousands of solar systems opposed the Republic under the leadership of Count Dooku, who was secretly Darth Sidious's apprentice. Many senators believed in a diplomatic solution, but the Galactic Senate debated about the creation of an army that would put an end to a frail peace.

JEDI GUARDIANS

Padmé Amidala, now a senator of the Republic, survived an assassination attempt. While a grown-up Anakin Skywalker was assigned the task of protecting her, Obi-Wan Kenobi traveled to the mysterious planet Kamino beyond the Outer Rim. There, he discovered a clone army was being developed in secret, created for the Republic's defense.

BIRTH OF AN EMPIRE

FIRST STEP

During a mission to free Supreme Chancellor Palpatine from capture by the Separatists, Obi-Wan Kenobi and Anakin Skywalker—now a Jedi Knight—faced Count Dooku aboard General Grievous's flagship. Obi-Wan was rendered unconscious during the battle, leaving Anakin to fight Dooku alone. Anakin disarmed the Sith Lord and, encouraged by Palpatine, delivered a final, killing blow.

53 BSI

BATTLE OF GEONOSIS

Supreme Chancellor Palpatine was given emergency powers to defend the Republic and engage the Separatists. To strike Count Dooku's forces, the clone army was deployed for the first time. Under the command of the Jedi, the army fought on the planet Geonosis. The battle was won, but a war had started.

THE DREAM

Anakin Skywalker learned Padmé Amidala was pregnant with his child. Not long after, he dreamed about her dying in childbirth and feared that the dream would become true. Supreme Chancellor Palpatine told Anakin the story of Darth Plagueis, a Sith Lord so powerful he mastered the ability to stop death.

TURNED TO THE DARK SIDE

Supreme Chancellor Palpatine revealed he was Darth Sidious, apprentice of Darth Plagueis and holder of his secrets. Desperate not to lose his only chance to save Padmé Amidala, Anakin Skywalker helped Sidious defeat Mace Windu, irrevocably turning to the dark side and becoming Darth Vader.

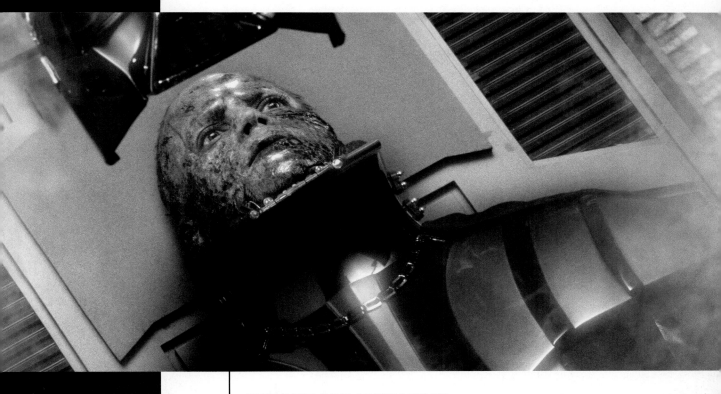

THE RISE OF DARTH VADER

Obi-Wan Kenobi confronted and defeated his former apprentice, almost killing him. As Emperor Palpatine rescued Darth Vader and gave him a life-sustaining suit of armor, Padmé Amidala died giving birth to twins: Luke Skywalker and Leia Organa.

34 BSI

NO MORE JEDI

Across the galaxy, the clone troopers followed Emperor Palpatine's directive, Order 66, and attacked their Jedi generals. Yoda and and Obi-Wan Kenobi seemed to be the only survivors. With no one left to stop him, Palpatine reorganized the Republic into the first Galactic Empire.

THE REBELLION

Leia Organa, known as Princess Leia, was raised unaware of her origin, by Bail Organa, the senator from the planet Alderaan. Bail helped form the Rebel Alliance, a group of freedom fighters dedicated to restoring the Republic.

THE PLANS

A group of rebels stole the plans to an incredibly powerful Imperial battle station called the Death Star. While carrying the plans, Princess Leia's consular ship the *Tantive IV* was was captured by Darth Vader and his troops.

MASTER OF EVIL

Before Luke Skywalker, Han Solo, and the other left the Death Star, Obi-Wan Kenobi engaged in duel with Darth Vader. To help Luke and the other escape, Obi-Wan let himself be killed by his forme apprentice, now a master of evil.

LUKE SKYWALKER

Princess Leia placed the plans to the Death Star inside the memory banks of astromech droid R2-D2. Along with protocol droid C-3PO, R2 escaped the Empire and landed on the planet Tatooine. R2's mission was to locate Obi-Wan Kenobi and deliver the coveted information to him, but he met Luke Skywalker first.

SAVING THE PRINCESS

R2-D2 managed to reach Obi-Wan Kenobi, who was now known by the name of Ben Kenobi. The old Jedi Knight, along with Luke; smuggler Han Solo; and his copilot, Chewbacca, infiltrated the Death Star and saved Princess Leia.

THE BATTLE OF YAVIN

Princess Leia and her rescuers arrived at the rebel base, located in the Yavin system. The analysis of the stolen plans revealed a weakness in the Death Star. When the battle station approached, the rebels attacked. Guided by the Force, Luke Skywalker destroyed the Death Star.

THE END OF THE EMPIRE

FACING THE EMPEROR

Luke Skywalker left his friends and surrendered to Darth Vader, giving up his lightsaber. Luke believed there was still good in his father and wanted to turn him back to the light side. Vader nevertheless took him to Emperor Palpatine.

31 BSI

THE TRAINING

Luke Skywalker learned the ways of the Force on the planet Dagobah, under the guidance of Jedi Master Yoda. Meanwhile, Han Solo and Princess Leia fell into a trap on the gas mining colony of Cloud City. Luke had a vision of this event during his training.

FATHER AND SON

Eager to rescue his friends, Luke Skywalker confronted Darth Vader in Cloud City. In the epic duel, Luke discovered Vader was his father, Anakin Skywalker. The Sith Lord severed Luke's hand, but the young Jedi survived the fight.

SECRET ATTACK

Yoda died, and a second, even more powerful Death Star was being built. The rebels planned to destroy it, but the station was protected by an impenetrable shield. Luke Skywalker, Princess Leia, Han Solo, and Chewbacca landed on the nearby forest moon of Endor and headed to the shield generator.

THE END OF "THE NEW REPUBLIC"

A MASTER DISAPPEARS

Luke Skywalker started to train a new generation of Jedi, but one of his apprentices, his nephew, Ben Solo—son of Leia and Han—turned against him. Led by fear and anger, Ben slaughtered the other students and destroyed the Jedi temple. He became Kylo Ren. Feeling responsible, Luke vanished.

30 BSI

THE BATTLE OF ENDOR

Emperor Palpatine failed to turn Luke Skywalker to the dark side and resolved to kill him. Luke called for his father's help, and and Darth Vader threw Emperor Palpatine into the Death Star reactor shaft. Anakin Skywalker had redeemed himself and died saving his son. Meanwhile, on Endor, the shield was deactivated, and the rebels destroyed the second Death Star. The Empire was brought to the brink of destruction.

A NEW ORDER

Corruption and darkness infected the Galactic Senate. The First Order, a military and political organization inspired by the Empire, extended its sphere of influence. Supreme Leader Snoke aimed for total domination.

THE RESISTANCE

Unwilling to let the First Order prevail, Leia Organa, now a general, led a movement of freedom fighters: the Resistance. In need of her brother Luke Skywalker's help, who had mysteriously disappeared, Leia sent her best pilot, Poe Dameron, to the desert planet Jakku in hopes of recovering part of a map that would help lead them to Luke's location.

DESERT ADVENTURE

In the Jakku desert, BB-8 was rescued by a young scavenger named Rey. Together with Finn, a former stormtrooper who left the First Order and set Poe Dameron free, Rey and BB-8 left Jakku on a stolen vessel, the *Millennium Falcon*. Their mission was to take the information to the Resistance.

0 BSI

THE MAP

Seeking the same map, the First Order sent multiple transports filled with stormtroopers to Jakku. Poe Dameron was captured by Kylo Ren, but the Resistance ace managed to pass the information to BB-8, his loyal astromech droid.

PIRATE HELP

The *Millennium Falcon* was captured by its former owners, Han Solo and Chewbacca. Along with Rey, Finn, and BB-8, they reached the planet Takodana seeking the help of pirate legend Maz Kanata. Anakin Skywalker's lost lightsaber called to Rey, and she was revealed to be strong with the Force.

A SINGLE SHOT

Starkiller Base, a planet converted into a superweapon, destroyed the Hosnian system, including the capital planet, Hosnian Prime, the Galactic Senate, and its defense fleet. The Resistance was left alone to confront the military might of the First Order.

FIRST DUEL

The Force awakened in Rey, and she managed to defeat Kylo Ren in a frantic lightsaber duel after he severely injured Finn. When Poe Dameron destroyed Starkiller Base the planet started to collapse. Rey and Finn were rescued by Chewbacca, while Kylo was rescued by First Order general, Armitage Hux.

0 ASI

THE BATTLE OF TAKODANA

The First Order attacked Takodana in search of the map. Captured by Kylo Ren, Rey was brought to Starkiller Base for questioning. Ren tried to read her mind, but Rey resisted. Meanwhile, Poe Dameron and a squadron of Resistance starfighters saved Finn, BB-8, Han Solo, and Chewbacca.

FATHER AND SON

On the planet D'Qar, site of the Resistance base, General Leia Organa planned to attack Starkiller Base. Han Solo, Chewbacca, and Finn volunteered to infiltrate and disable the enemy's defensive shield. Later, Han confronted his son and told him it was not too late to abandon the dark side. Kylo Ren then killed Solo.

FAR FROM THE FORCE

Using the combined maps held by BB-8 and R2-D2, Rey arrived on the planet Ahch-To, where she persuaded Luke Skywalker to teach her the ways of the Force. During her time, Rey experienced a Force connection with Kylo Ren.

BUILDING A NEW REBELLION

TO THE LAST SHIP

Rey left Ahch-To, convinced there was still conflict in Kylo Ren. Meanwhile, the Resistance fleet could not escape Supreme Leader Snoke and his flagship, now able to track any vessel through hyperspace. The ships were destroyed one by one until only a warship remained.

LAST HOPE

SECRET MISSION

Finn and Rose, a Resistance mechanic, were sent to the casino city of Canto Bight on the planet Cantonica. There, they sought the Master Codebreaker and then snuck aboard the First Order flagship to disable the tracking device. The mission failed, and Finn and Rose were captured.

FOR A LIGHTSABER

Rey surrendered herself to Kylo Ren, who then took her before Supreme Leader Snoke. Ordered to execute Rey, Kylo Ren instead killed the Supreme Leader and defeated his Praetorian Guard, fighting side by side with Rey. After failing to turn him to the light, Rey left. Kylo Ren then proclaimed himself the new Supreme Leader.

Vice Admiral Holdo sacrificed herself to destroy the First Order's flagship, which enabled the remaining survivors to reach the planet Crait. Finn, Rose Tico, and BB-8 soon arrived on the planet, as well, but so did the First Order. Luke Skywalker, who Force-projected himself onto the planet, engaged Kylo Ren in a duel. Afterwards, Luke became one with the Force, but his actions allowed the remaining Resistance fighters to escape aboard the *Millennium Falcon*.

THE FINAL ORDER

Thanks to a wayfinder device, Supreme Leader Ren got to the mysterious planet Exegol where he met Emperor Palpatine, alive but debilitated. Palpatine revealed to Kylo Ren that he had been behind Snoke and the First Order since the beginning. In exchange for the power to rule the galaxy—an unrivaled fleet called Final Order—he also asked Kylo Ren to kill Rey.

1 ASI

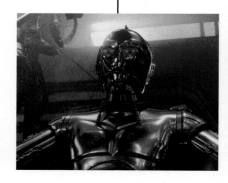

SEARCHING FOR EXEGOL

The Resistance learned about Palpatine and his fleet in an encrypted message from a First Order spy but didn't know where Exegol was. In the Jedi texts she took from Ahch-To, Rey read that Luke Skywalker had known about the mysterious planet and had tried to hunt down a Sith wayfinder to reach it. Together with Poe Dameron, Chewbacca, Finn, BB-8, and C-3PO, Rey thus left for planet Pasaana to resume the search.

THE DAGGER

On Pasaana, Rey found a dagger inscribed with Sith language, which gave the coordinates to the wayfinder. C-3PO could translate them, but couldn't reveal the translation due to programming restrictions. In order to hack his memory, Rey and the others took him on planet Kijimi. Searching for Rey, Kylo Ren also arrived on Kijimi.

PALPATINE'S LINEAGE

In a confrontation with Kylo Ren, Rey finally learned the truth about her lineage: she was Emperor Palpatine's granddaughter. The young Jedi was shocked but managed to escape from Kylo Ren, refusing to join him. With her friends, as C-3PO indicated, she then got to Kef Bir, a moon in the Endor system. The Sith wayfinder was hidden there, inside the ruins of the Second Death Star.

SAVING THE GALAXY

MASTER SKYWALKER

After she took Kylo Ren's ship, Rey traveled to planet Ahch-To, to live there in exile. But Luke Skywalker's Force ghost appeared and prompted her to face Palpatine. Given Leia Organa's lightsaber—for also the late princess trained as a Jedi— and using Kylo Ren's wayfinder found on his ship, Rey left for Exegol. Meanwhile, remembering his father, Ben Solo turned to the light.

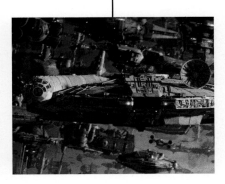

THE DUEL

Touching the device, Rey had a vision of herself as a Sith. Moments later, Kylo Ren appeared and destroyed the wayfinder. The only way to reach Exegol was with him now. A fierce duel followed. Before he could defeat Rey, Leia Organa connected with her son through the Force, right before dying. This gave Rey the opportunity to stab him. Sensing Leia's death, though, Rey decided to heal Kylo Ren using the Force.

THE BATTLE OF EXEGOL

Following Rey's signal, the Resistance fleet reached Exegol and engaged in battle with the Final Order. Inside the Sith citadel, Rey and Ben Solo faced the Emperor, but Palpatine absorbed their exceptional lifeforce and rejuvenated, gaining enough power to defeat them and stop the Resistance fleet's attack. Strengthened by the spirit of past Jedi, Rey managed to stand up.

THE RISE OF SKYWALKER

Using both Skywalkers' lightsabers to divert Palpatine's attack, Rey killed him and died. Ben Solo then sacrificed himself to revive Rey, who kissed him before his death. Above them, the Resistance fleet won the battle with the help of reinforcements from all over the galaxy. The war to the rising new Empire was finally over. Later on, Rey buried the Skywalker lightsabers on Tatooine and took their name as hers.

REY

MORE THAN A SCAVENGER

2 /

Bold and independent, but with a generous heart, nineteen-year-old Rey lived alone on the remote planet Jakku. She scavenged valuable technology from wrecks in a spaceship graveyard, then sold it for food at Niima Outpost. One day, Rey helped a small droid in need, beginning a journey that took her a long way from Jakku and from who she had always thought she was.

ALONE IN THE GALAXY

The moment she touched Anakin Skywalker's lightsaber in Maz Kanata's castle on Takodana, Rey received a series of visions. In one of them, Rey saw herself as a child yelling out to a starship taking off, begging it to come back. From that moment on, she had grown up alone.

"Rey comes from an isolated community," says Lawrence Kasdan, co-writer of *The Force Awakens* (2015), *The Empire Strikes Back* (1980), and *Return of the Jedi* (1983). "Her emotional life has been isolated.

A young woman living alone on a remote planet.

She doesn't have the support of family. She doesn't have friends." And that is the direction in which the story took her, along with the audience. "Family is what *Star Wars* is all about," recalls actress Daisy Ridley, who plays Rey. "The family thing translated everywhere. Even on set, it felt like a family. It's that feeling of bonding, everywhere. Rey is trying to find her place in this world in the same way I was trying to find my place in the world. The similarities were really nice. Because I felt so welcomed, and taken in, and people seemed to care how I felt, that translated into Rey. She suddenly had these people who cared about her, and she was finding her place within that."

3 /

LIFE ON JAKKU

The harsh conditions on Jakku taught Rey that she couldn't let her guard down. She had to be always ready to fight, because bullies only fear strength. Not a trained soldier, not yet a Jedi, Rey's fighting skills were nevertheless amazing. "Because her background was scavenging and resourcing, reclaiming bits and pieces," explains Rob Inch, the film's stunt coordinator, "she would be naturally physical but would not look like a martial artist. So we made her fighting more scrappy and physical. Then, as we got through the movie and developed her more with the lightsaber, it was something within her rather than something that she was trained for." Ridley trained four days a week, five hours a day to look like a scavenger who worked, ran, climbed, and fought almost every day of her life: "I was really pleased from a personal standpoint. Rey is an emotionally strong female character, which is amazing. I had never climbed before, I had never done any kind of fight-training before. All of it was such an amazing feeling."

A NATURAL

During her life as a scavenger, Rey became a very adept mechanic. She built her own speeder, a model halfway between a speeder bike and a swoop, for travel across the Jakku landscape. Creature concept designer Jake Lunt Davies helped develop the design, together with his team: "All the way through the design process, the one thing I kept bearing in mind was the simplicity to silhouettes and shapes. If you look at the original films, so many of the iconic elements can be sketched with a line. A Star Destroyer is a triangle; the Death Star is a circle with another circle in it; Darth Vader is this shape with a triangle. You can distill them down to very simple shapes. And Rey's speeder is a rectangle. A big rectangle on its side."

AMAZING SKILLS

Having worked with spacecraft from a young age, Rey was also an incredibly talented pilot. In the above concept painting by concept artist Doug Chiang (realized during the July 2013 preproduction phase), we see the *Millennium Falcon* under Rey's command flying through the wreckage of a Super Star Destroyer. "She had never flown anything like that before," said Ridley of the moment. "But she used what she knew to get out of the situation and start her journey."

5 /

4 /

1 / Rey with her staff, outside the junkyard settlement of Niima Outpost on Jakku. (See previous spread)

2 / Uncovering Anakin Skywalker's lightsaber in Maz Kanata's castle on Takodana. (See previous spread)

3 / The final version of Rey in a concept painting by Glyn Dillon.

4 / Rey travels across the Jakku desert aboard her home-made speeder.

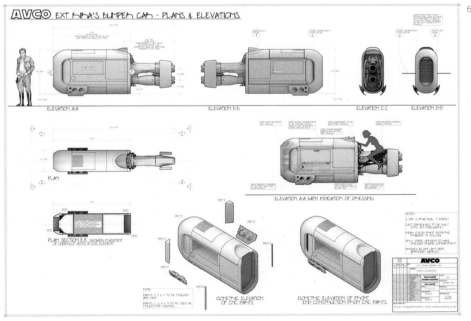

5 / The *Millennium Falcon* flies inside the wreckage of a Super Star Destroyer, by concept artist Doug Chiang.

6 / Plans and elevations for Rey's speeder by draughtsman Andrew Proctor.

THE FORCE

Kylo Ren and his master, Supreme Leader Snoke, felt a sudden awakening in the Force for the first time since the disappearance of Luke Skywalker. It was only when Ren tried to read Rey's mind, and she resisted, that they both realized the Force was trying to connect with a young scavenger, a nobody. Later in the film, during the lightsaber duel on Starkiller Base, Kylo Ren told Rey he could show her the ways of the Force. Those words resonated with her, as Ridley explains: "He pushed her to find her strength. He pushed her into a place she had never been before. The fear and anger of what he was doing. He mentioned Han Solo. And, because he had become like a father figure to Rey, it affected her. Her thought was, 'I'm not going to take this, I'm going to find my strength.' And she did."

7 /

The Force was trying to connect with a young scavenger, a nobody.

SALVAGED WEAPON

According to Toby Wagner, chargehand propmaker for the film, the staff Rey used in the Jakku desert was made with old engine parts and pieces from a lathe, but it was too heavy for the stunts. So the props department made it lighter, scanning the original and reducing it down to the right size.

HOME

Rey lived in the belly of an Imperial AT-AT walker, one of the many remnants of the Galactic Civil War. According to set decorator Lee Sandales, this was one of the smaller sets. Inside it, they put three details that helped illuminate Rey's life: a Rebel Alliance pilot doll she crafted when she was ten years old, a cooker made out of bits of the engine, and a desert flower. "Rey had never seen a really beautiful, living flower," says Sandales. "She lived in a world where there was no water." ☮

7 / Rey engages Kylo Ren in a lightsaber duel in the forest on Starkiller Base.

8 / Rey sitting outside her AT-AT walker home on Jakku.

9 / Rey's goggles are made with stormtrooper helmet lenses.

10 / The Rebel Alliance pilot doll Rey crafted from debris she found.

DESERT OUTFIT

Rey's costume, which protects her from the heat and the wind, was very simple. Short trousers, a T-shirt made out of a cotton jersey, a very long strip of silk fabric, and goggles on top. To age it, and make it suit the Jakku environment, the costume department painted and sprayed color onto it.

FINN
MORE THAN A TROOPER

1 /

His previous name was just a serial number, FN-2187, and he was trained by the First Order to be a stormtrooper. Despite his excellent results in combat simulations, he was not prepared for a real, brutal battlefield. Sent to Jakku under the leadership of Captain Phasma, he had a change of heart and became a fugitive. Unlike his fellow stormtroopers, FN-2187's good nature couldn't be suppressed.

RAISED TO OBEY

Most stormtroopers who were in the First Order's army were taken away from their families and conscripted against their will at a very young age. They were raised to do what they were told, to kill whom they were told to kill, and not to ever question authority. And because most were there against their will, they couldn't rely on anyone but their fellow squad mates. "Very much like Rey, Finn was alone," said Lawrence Kasdan, writer of *The*

Stormtrooper FN-2187 was not prepared for the reality of battle.

Force Awakens. "All he knew was comradery could be derived from his fellow troopers. But he had a crisis of conscience. He started thinking, rebelling against the idea that he would be the killing apparatus for something he didn't understand. And that's the moment we met him. When he was so shocked by the actions of his leader, he couldn't take part." On Jakku, the First Order slaughtered all the Tuanul villagers while they tried to fight back. In the crossfire, some troopers were hit. Unable to help his comrades, because he was reluctant to kill the enemies, FN-2187 pretended his blaster was jammed. This was the first act of his desertion.

1 / First Order
stormtroopers attack
the village of Tuanul,
on the planet Jakku.
(See previous spread)

2 / FN-2187, renamed
Finn, at the junkyard
settlement of Niima
Outpost. (See previous
spread)

3 / FN-2187 frees Poe
Dameron from his cell
and asks for his help.

4 / Finn wears Poe
Dameron's jacket in
this concept painting
by Glyn Dillon. "We
added a pilot look
to the sleeve," says
costume supervisor
Dave Crossman,
"which was an
homage to *Star Wars*
and Luke's jacket in
*The Empire Strikes
Back*."

FACELESS NO MORE

Armored stormtroopers had been the symbol of the Imperial presence across the galaxy. They then became the symbol of the First Order's military might. The infantry helmet they wore concealed any shred of individuality. FN-2187 was just a number. But under the mask there was someone who was confused, frightened, and full of other emotions. "This idea that there was a guy underneath the uniform that became a main character in the film, and one of our central heroes, was really interesting," recalled director J.J. Abrams. "The only time we had seen people in stormtrooper uniforms was when Luke and Han put them on to help save Leia [in *Star Wars: A New Hope*]. It felt like a great beginning of something. It connected thematically to this idea of, 'Who are these people behind these masks?' All the new characters were masked. Kylo Ren was masked, Rey was masked when you first met her, and Finn too. He was part of something evil and insidious and violent, but he had something undeniable—a conscience. He knew it was wrong. And how and what to do about it was completely unknown to him. It felt like a really compelling story in any universe, but in *Star Wars*, it just felt like an amazing thing."

4 /

3 /

"Poe gave Finn hope. Poe gave him a direct link to good."

JOHN BOYEGA

A NEW NAME

Back on the Star Destroyer *Finalizer*, FN-2187 and captive Resistance pilot Poe Dameron hastily conceived an escape plan. Used to improvisation, Poe followed FN-2187's lead and agreed to steal a Special Forces TIE fighter from the docking bay. During their daring escape, Poe gave FN-2187 a real name and a new identity: Finn. "For him, that was his first connection with good," said actor John Boyega, who played Finn. "The first time he fought for something positive. That changed him. In general, you found Finn becoming a man. From a boy who took orders, who didn't know about substance, and what it meant to be good, to a man who understood what good was, and willing to fight

for it." After crash-landing in the Sinking Fields of the Goazon Badlands on Jakku, Finn was separated from Poe, fearing his new friend may indeed be dead. Trying to stay out of sight, he took his armor off and wore Poe's jacket. "What this jacket symbolized to Finn, and what I played internally," continued Boyega, "is that this was his connection to something good. You wouldn't find a member of the First Order wearing that jacket. People who saw him dressed like that would think, 'He's Resistance. He's fighting for the good of the galaxy.' Poe gave Finn hope. Poe gave him a direct link to good. And the jacket stayed with him for the rest of the movie, and became his."

5 / After crash-landing on Jakku, Finn wears Poe Dameron's jacket after leaving his stormtrooper armor behind.

INSEPARABLE

When Finn and Rey met for the first time, she ran after him and slammed him to the ground with her staff, thinking he was a thief. He had no other choice than to lie and tell Rey he was with the Resistance. Finn didn't believe he was a hero, but he could be one. He just needed to find something, or someone, worth fighting for. As the film continued, Rey became that someone. "What was so special about those two is that they came from different worlds, but their cause, their situation, and the circumstances were the same," said Boyega. "They wanted to figure out where they fit in. Meeting each other, they found purpose. They found companionship. Then they found a reason to search for something bigger. Through BB-8, they were made aware of something amazing, and it made their bond inseparable."

6 / "Are you okay?" Finn asks Rey after a First Order TIE fighter attacks them.

7 / Finn behind the controls of the *Millennium Falcon* quad laser cannons.

7 /

"I CAN DO THIS"

On Jakku, Rey, Finn, and BB-8 stole the *Millennium Falcon* to escape two TIE fighters. Finn took the gunner seat and, although the Corellian AG-2G quad laser cannons were stuck in forward position, he put his training to good use and shot down their pursuers. The *Falcon* hadn't been flown in years, and everything contributed to this feeling. "When Finn was sitting in the gunner seat and moved the turret, it had a rusty spin to it," said supervising sound editor David Accord. "You could hear the rust and grit fall off the cannon as it hit its endpoints. When it finally blasted for the first time it was a real awakening of this ship that had been dormant for who knows how many years."

8 /

STANDARD STORMTROOPER   SNOWTROOPER   FLAMETROOPER

JEDI SABER

After killing his father, Kylo Ren chased Rey and Finn out of Starkiller Base and confronted them in a snow-covered forest. Using the Force, Kylo knocked Rey unconscious and goaded Finn into a fight. The former stormtrooper used Anakin Skywalker's lightsaber and attacked him. But Finn was no match for Kylo Ren. According to Boyega, the lightsabers they used were very heavy: "I was able to get a sense of the power, the Force, that was coming out of the weapon." ☾

8 / As visualized in these paintings of First Order stormtroopers by concept artist Glyn Dillon, there is an appropriate class of soldier for any situation: standard stormtroopers; snowtroopers, deployed in subzero climates; and flametroopers armed with lethal incendiary weapons.

9 / Finn ignites Skywalker's lightsaber, ready to fight Kylo Ren on Starkiller Base.

1

POE DAMERON

ACE PILOT, RELENTLESS SOLDIER

2 /

Commander Poe Dameron was the most daring and skilled pilot in the Resistance. Born toward the end of the war between the Rebel Alliance and the Galactic Empire, he was raised on Yavin 4—the moon the rebels launched their attack from that destroyed the first Death Star. General Leia Organa, who had trust in Poe, sent him on a mission to retrieve information that would hopefully reveal Luke Skywalker's location.

MISSION ACCOMPLISHED

Together with his loyal droid, BB-8, Poe Dameron reached Tuanul, a small, remote village on Jakku, and received part of a map from an old Resistance ally, Lor San Tekka, to aid in the search for Luke. But when the First Order stormtroopers attacked the village, Poe had no other option than to entrust the secret information to BB-8 and send him away before being captured. Tortured by the First Order, Poe didn't

> ## "He's a fast pilot, a fast talker, someone who lived with death very close by."
> OSCAR ISAAC

reveal any information. He wasn't even intimidated by Kylo Ren when the dark warrior appeared.

"That's who Poe is," says actor Oscar Isaac, who played Poe Dameron. "He's a fast pilot, a fast talker, someone who lived with death very close by and went towards death as a good warrior should. He was the first one to throw himself in harm's way. That's something that I really liked, and I talked to J.J. a lot about. How to really find something simple and clear, but do it really strongly."

1 / Squadron leader
Poe Dameron wearing
his flight vest with the
Rebel Alliance symbol.
(See previous spread)

2 / Poe and FN-2187
steal a Special Forces
TIE fighter to escape.
(See previous spread)

3 / Poe Dameron
wearing his jacket
and village outfit as
imagined by concept
artist Glyn Dillon.

4 / Finn believes
Poe to be dead, until
he meets him on D'Qar.

5 / Poe aboard his
Black One during
the attack on
Starkiller Base.

3 /

LIKE BROTHERS

Freed from his cell by a stormtrooper, FN-2187, the
two stole a Special Forces TIE fighter from the main
hangar aboard a First Order Star Destroyer, flying
toward Jakku and through a barrage of cannon
fire and missiles from the massive starship. A close
bond between the two fugitives was formed, and
the stormtrooper became Finn, soon to become
a Resistance fighter. "John Boyega is a fantastic
human being," recalls Isaac. "He reminded me a
lot of my little brother, and that's a little bit of the
relationship that Poe and Finn had. We just laughed
a lot, and talked a lot about our scenes together. He
was incredibly flexible and on his toes with different
ideas." Hit by a missile, the TIE fighter crashed on
Jakku. Finn found himself alone in the middle of
an endless desert. There was no sign of Poe, and
when the ship sank into the sand and exploded, Finn
believed the Resistance pilot to be dead.

4 /

POE LIVES

The First Order attacked Maz Kanata's castle on Takodana. Finn, Han Solo, and Chewbacca were captured. But a Resistance squadron of starfighters arrived, led by Poe Dameron's X-wing, *Black One*. He was alive, and had indeed survived the crash-landing on Jakku. According to Isaac, originally the character was going to die in that crash. "This idea that Poe came back was something that was added later, which, obviously, for me, was incredibly exciting and fantastic—I got to live. Not only did

I find out that I got to live, but that I would come back in a black X-wing, which was the coolest thing I had ever heard in my life." Poe lived to become a symbol of the Resistance, one of its most important commanders, and his relationship with Finn evolved, defining both characters. "Poe lived," explained director J.J. Abrams, "and he lived partly because Oscar questioned it. He's spectacular in the movie. And I loved where he went in the next episode. I just adore Oscar, and I loved working with him. He brought an incredible strength to this heroic role."

6 / The TIE fighter crash site as imagined by concept artist Andrée Wallin in this painting from October 2013. The damaged model of the First Order fighter seen in the film was built in Pinewood Studios, England, then taken to the Abu Dhabi desert, United Arab Emirates, where the scene was shot.

6 /

7 / Poe Dameron
wearing his flight
suit as imagined
by concept artist
Glyn Dillon.

8 / The Resistance
X-wing squadron
flying in the Takodana
atmosphere.

7 /

> "It was unlike
> anything I
> had ever done
> before."
>
> OSCAR ISAAC

THE REAL THING

Poe's starfighter was a customized Incom-FreiTek T-70, the one and only black X-wing in the Resistance fleet. Working on the set with practical starfighter models was very important for the actors. "We had two full-sized X-wings we could run up to," said Isaac. "The cockpits were open and we could just jump into them. I think everyone who was on set felt like they were real. And being able to literally run through the sand and up to my X-wing was unlike anything I had ever done before."

RESISTANCE FLEET

The X-wings were a most useful weapon in the hands of the Resistance, who had to rely on hit-and-run tactics when they faced the First Order. According to senior art director Gary Tomkins, most of the techniques used to create the ships, as well as the speeders, were the same used more than 40 years ago for the first *Star Wars* films: "The X-wing fuselage was carved out of polystyrene by modelers. Molds were made in the plaster shop, in the way they've been made for many years. The technique of construction, the painting of the models, was all exactly the same. A lot of the little details were found items. We went through yards and yards of aircraft salvage, and found little pieces. Then we spray painted them, put them on the fuselage, and the result was something better than you can even imagine."

REBEL EQUIPMENT

Poe's mother was an Alliance fighter pilot; his father served in the rebel military. On his helmet, Poe wore an old Rebel Alliance symbol. Even the design of the quadnoculars he used to spot the First Order on Jakku was reminiscent of that earlier era. "Because Poe had a rebel background," explained prop master Jamie Wilkinson, "we thought we'd try to design equipment that had that look and feel. We started with a set of weapons that was close to where we left off in *Return of the Jedi*—rebel blasters, rifles, and pistols that were all in that old-school vein. Then, we re-imagined those as modern versions of the rebel weapons, designed thirty years later after the events of *Return*."

9 / Poe Dameron posing in front of his black X-wing on D'Qar.

10 / Dameron's Neuro-Saav TE 4.4 field quadnoculars.

10 /

BB-8

ROLLING FOR THE RESISTANCE

1/

A spherical astromech droid, equipped to control the flight and power distribution systems of a starfighter, BB-8 was also a trusted Resistance agent and the loyal, enthusiastic sidekick of pilot Poe Dameron. This little droid would face any danger to stay close to his companion. Agile and particularly fast, BB-8 usually tried to go unnoticed, as his self-preservation protocols required.

A SPHERE WITH A HEART

BB-8 controlled his body—made of six circular tool-bay disks—through wireless telemetry. An internal orbiculate motivator rolled him, while magnetic casters kept his head still. A significant amount of engineering, puppetry skills, and technology were required to create this droid in practice. As creative supervisor for creature effects and special make-up effects Neal Scanlan explained, bringing BB-8 to life was not without a significant number of challenges. "BB-8 is based on the most technological way of conceiving how a droid could navigate its way around the world." The drive systems that enabled BB-8 to

> ## "The meeting of Rey and BB-8 was hilarious... you know they will have a special bond."
>
> DAISY RIDLEY

move were particularly challenging, especially when compared to other droids like R2-D2. "A trolley, like R2-D2, has three wheels," continued Scanlan. "When it turns, there's a sort of algorithm of what wheel is driving at what speed. To accomplish the same thing with BB-8 without the trolley was incredibly difficult. And some motion was achieved by literally pushing BB-8 along like a wheelbarrow! A performer pushed the ball to roll, and controlled the attitude of the droid's head. So, it was a combination of simple puppetry skills and a lot of technology.

2

NEW FRIEND

Running away from the First Order stormtroopers, BB-8 was caught by a Teedo scavenger. The creature wanted the droid for its parts, but Rey wasn't far away. She heard BB-8's call for help and came to his aid. BB-8's language was a twenty-seventh-generation variant of the common astromech language, but a scavenger like Rey, who knew how machines worked, was familiar with nonhuman languages. The meeting of Rey and BB-8 was key to unlocking a particular aspect of Rey's character. As actress Daisy Ridley, who played Rey explained, "She instinctively saved BB-8 from the scavenger, didn't think anything of it. But when the droid looked into her eyes... I don't think anyone had ever looked at her that way before. From that point on, they have a special bond. He was her talisman, the first constant in Rey's life." The relationship was so important to Ridley, that she asked the director for more screen time together. "I asked J.J. If I could have more interaction with BB-8 because it was such a nice relationship. I didn't want it to be lost."

1 / On Jakku, BB-8 sees the First Order troops approach from the sky and attack the Tuanul village.

2 / Rey fixes BB-8's high-frequency receiver antenna in the Takodana forest.

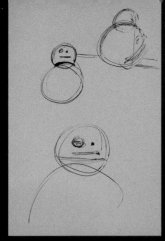
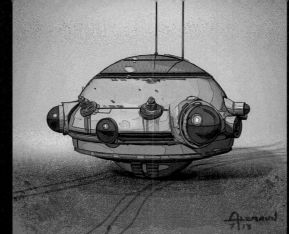
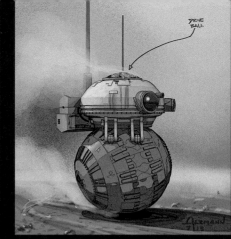

3 / Starting from J.J.
Abrams' sketch,
concept artist Christian
Alzmann imagines
BB-8 for the first
time as seen in these
paintings from
summer 2013.

4 / Finn, Rey, and BB-8
in the corridor of the
Millennium Falcon.

4 /

"BB-8 became something that felt right very quickly."

J.J. ABRAMS

ON SET

The BB-8 seen in the film was a nearly 100 percent practical character, played by different units. One was the puppeteered version, controlled by puppeteers Brian Herring and Dave Chapman. "That version was fantastic for close-ups," recalled animatronic designer Josh Lee, "and when you really wanted a subtle, emotive performance. It was also great for terrible terrain, because Brian could run BB-8 over deserts, woods, and tree roots." In addition to this version, there were also two the production team referred to as "trikes." "The two radio-controlled trikes had small wheels to help stabilize BB-8," Lee said. "That was good for situations where we didn't really want Brian blocking the actors, or where BB-8 was more incidental to the scene, but we still needed him to roam through the set. There were two trikes, so we could shoot from two different sides." Another version, known as "the wiggler," served an entirely different purpose. "You never see the wiggler roam around," Lee said, "but we could shoot all around it without CGI [computer-generate imagery], and it would give a good performance." Other iterations of BB-8 included a stunt version that could be dropped into a shot, a "carrier" version that was lighter than the others so it could be easily picked up, and a "bowling ball" version. "That was great fun," Lee said, referring to the "bowling ball" BB-8. "It was weighted at the bottom, on casters, and you could bowl it through the frame if you wanted a madcap BB-8, whizzing and pirouetting through the frame! There were some funny shots in the *Millennium Falcon* when we were doing that."

GALACTIC HELPERS

Astromech droids provided onboard flight support to the Resistance forces. They carried out a variety of mechanical repair and power control tasks, but they also accompanied starfighters as copilots. BB-8, for example, always made sure the settings on Poe Dameron's X-wing were configured to his preferences.

THE NAME

"The name simply came out of an onomatopoeic," recalled director J.J. Abrams. "It was the first name I had for him. I didn't know if it would stick or not, and it just did. Even the word, the title, *Star Wars*, the first time I ever saw it was in *Starlog Magazine*, I remember saying it out loud because I'd never heard it before. It sounded weird to me. It's amazing how quickly it can go from something you hear for the first time, to being what it is. BB-8 became something that felt right very quickly." ☺

5 / BB-8 aboard Poe Dameron's *Black One* during the attack against Starkiller Base.

6 / Poe and BB-8 meet again on D'Qar after they are separated on Jakku.(Next spread)

KYLO REN

ON THE DARK SIDE

1 /

Impulsive and ruthless, Kylo Ren was lost in anger and hate. Through his veins ran the bloodline of the most powerful Jedi and Sith, for he was once Ben Solo, the son of Han Solo and Leia Organa, grandson of Darth Vader. A gifted Jedi and student of Luke Skywalker, Ben turned to the dark side of the Force, took a new name, and became the apprentice of Supreme Leader Snoke.

A CONFLICT

Kylo Ren was trying to become one with the dark side of the Force, immune to the light. But his journey was not yet complete. "The character of Kylo Ren was about becoming," said co-producer Michelle Rejwan. "He's not fully formed. He was on a journey to discover himself. To discover his full potential. In *Star Wars*, there's the light and the dark side of both of those things. Kylo Ren was striving to be some kind of force, and having both the light and the dark in him, was warring on both sides. That's what made the character so interesting to watch." Despite the

He was once Ben Solo, the son of Han Solo and Leia Organa.

effort to hide it, his inner conflict was evident when he exited his shuttle on Jakku and faced the captive Lor San Tekka—the explorer who was harboring part of a map to Luke Skywalker's location. As actor Adam Driver explained, that inner conflict, the becoming, showed in the character's visual presentation. "His lightsaber was not quite finished, and his uniform was not quite perfect." Lor San Tekka tells Kylo he cannot deny his past, his family, where he came from. As we would soon learn, Kylo's parents were Leia and Han. Well aware of Kylo's feelings towards his mother and father, Supreme Leader Snoke exploited his apprentice's battle with the light and the dark to his own advantage.

FROM THE PAST

Obsessed with Darth Vader, Kylo kept the deformed mask of the fallen Sith Lord in his private quarters aboard the *Finalizer*—a *Resurgent*-class Star Destroyer—and talked to it as if it were alive. Kylo emulated Vader, striving to be as strong as he was, even though Snoke believed Vader's weakness caused the end of the Empire. "It's very important," said Lawrence Kasdan, writer of *The Force Awakens*, "that Snoke, who's a master manipulator, could frame the moment of Anakin's redemption as Darth Vader's biggest failure, and have that argument carry total weight with Kylo Ren, who is now Snoke's protégée and servant. Someone else telling that story would talk about the great moment when Anakin was redeemed, and Luke did not give up on his father. But for Snoke, it represented Vader's moment of fatal weakness, when he softened at the end."

JUST A BOY

While Anakin Skywalker had to wear his mask to breathe, Kylo Ren didn't. His mask—designed after the battle gear of the Knights of Ren, a new generation devoted to the dark side—served the purpose of

> "His mask serves the purpose of intimidating his opponents and hiding his humanity."
>
> MATTHEW WOOD

4 /

5 /

intimidating his opponents and hiding his humanity. After taking Rey to Starkiller Base, Kylo Ren was ready to interrogate her. But first, he took off his mask and showed his face. What she saw took Rey by surprise. Kylo Ren was just a boy. "One of the most interesting things was he's young," said Kathleen Kennedy, Lucasfilm president. "So often, villains in stories are damaged, troubled, older characters. To bring a character into *Star Wars* as a villain who was only thirty years old was interesting. It took advantage of a troubled, teenage life, and a backstory that we didn't know much about. We recognized this tension between dark and light, which is prevalent in *Star Wars*, and we used it as a metaphor for the path from young adulthood to being an adult, to whom you think you'll be as an adult, what your aspirations might be. That interest in anything on the dark side. Anybody's capable of that. I think that tension of being drawn into something dangerous is relatable. For audiences today, that's a new and exciting and appealing character."

THE MASK

Kylo Ren's mask was part of his battered combat helmet. Servomotors could drive articulated arms to separate the mask from the helmet, letting Ren show his face to his opponents when needed. Supervising sound editor Matthew Wood and his team used the sound of chains to make Adam Driver's voice—when he is wearing the mask—as distorted and intimidating as possible: "The mask didn't function like Vader's mask to keep him alive. It was for intimidation and to make him very strange to interact with. The juxtaposition when he took the helmet off, his regular voice and face gave a nice yin-yang surprise effect."

1 / Kylo Ren's command shuttle as imagined by concept artist Ryan Church, in this painting from October 2013. The enormous stabilizer wings serve as deflector shield projection and sensor surfaces. (See previous spread)

2 / Kylo Ren leading the First Order stormtroopers on Jakku. (See previous spread)

3 / Ren aboard the *Resurgent*-class Star Destroyer, the *Finalizer*.

4 / Kylo Ren's battered combat helmet.

5 / Kylo Ren removes his mask to confront his father, Han Solo.

FIERY LIGHTSABER

Kylo Ren built his own-unconventional-lightsaber, and its design was unlike any other: it had a main red blade and two smaller crossguard blades, or quillons. The quillons, projected from the side, helped balance the power of the lightsaber and protect Kylo's hand. As director J.J. Abrams recalled: "The idea was that Kylo Ren had joined this group of knights, the Knights of Ren, and he built this lightsaber with them. But he built this thing without the proper guidance and training. He built one because he wanted one. The idea that he was good with it, and deadly with it, but not particularly trained and not a master of it was important."

RAW POWER

The blade was unstable; the hilt looked crudely assembled. It was a lightsaber, but it didn't look or sound like the other Jedi and Sith weapons. "Ren's saber had a pretty iconic sound," explained supervising sound editor David Accord. "It was raw, unstable. It didn't have the refined, smooth swish sound that Luke Skywalker's saber had. It sounded angry and animalistic. That's the way Kylo Ren was in the movie."

DUEL IN THE SNOW

According to Abrams, the lightsaber duel in the snow was one of the first things they wanted to do. "Partly because of how the blades would interact with the snow and the characters. With the original *Star Wars*, when the lightsabers came on, the light affected nothing around it. What was interesting, having the prop in this movie, was how much light actually did interact with the eyes, a face, the wardrobe of the characters. And I thought it would be a beautiful thing to do in the snow." The scene was shot in five days at Pinewood Studios, England, where a large snow forest set was built. ☾

7 /   8 /

9 /

6 / Searching for BB-8 and the map to Luke Skywalker on Takodana.

7 / Ren's lightsaber, the unstable plasma blade ignited.

8 / Concept artist Lee Oliver imagines the lightsaber for Kylo Ren in this painting from February 2014.

9 / Concept artist Christian Alzmann imagines a Jedi Killer (the main villain in an earlier version of the story) contemplating the melted helmet of Darth Vader, almost like Kylo Ren does in the film.

10 / After killing his father, Ren is about to attack Finn and Rey.

10 /

THE FORCE AWAKENS

THE FIRST ORDER

SUCCESSOR TO THE EMPIRE

An endless army of new stormtroopers, equipped with the finest weapons; a fleet of galactic Star Destroyers; a superweapon with the power to destroy an entire system. This is the First Order, the military organization that inherited the legacy, targets, and purposes of the Empire. Under the leadership of mysterious Supreme Leader Snoke, it planned to take control of the galaxy.

SUPREME LEADER SNOKE

As the Supreme Leader of the First Order, Snoke commanded his generals from his secret chambers— only projecting a large-scale version of himself. Powerful in the dark side of the Force, but not a Sith like the Emperor, Snoke acknowledged the might in Kylo Ren's blood and pulled him to the dark side of the Force. "Snoke watched the Galactic Empire rise and fall," said actor Andy Serkis, who played Snoke.

"Snoke could see Kylo Ren falling prey to his emotions..."

ANDY SERKIS

"He could see Kylo Ren falling prey to his emotions the way Anakin Skywalker did, and he wanted to guard against that at all costs. You could see this rising temper in Snoke, being squashed down and bottled, and you could see it coming alive. It was great to play, to suppress all of that. To not let that Pandora's Box open until a particular moment."

1 / The First Order troops gathered on Starkiller Base.

2 / Supreme Leader Snoke's hologram.

3 /

4 /

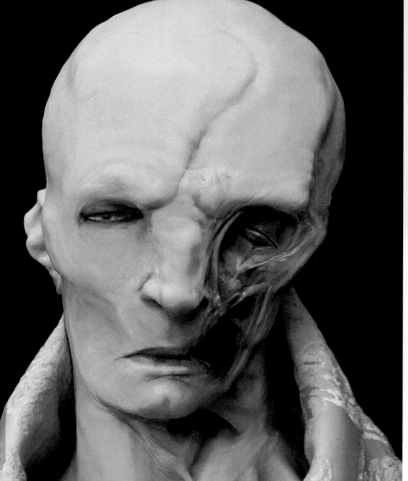

MOTION-CAPTURE ACTOR

Snoke's immense hologram hid his frail body, deceiving anyone who wasn't allowed to see him in the flesh. Because of the scale, the scenes in which Snoke appeared in the film were shot in motion capture. As Serkis explained: "It's the art and craft of an actor embodying a role that will be manifested on screen as a CGI character. Instead of putting on a costume and makeup beforehand, I played the role without the help of those things, but neither the hindrance. All of the facial expressions, all my acting decisions, and the authorship of the role happened on set with the other actors. Then, a team of animators and CGI artists had the job of transposing my performance onto a digital avatar without losing the nuance and subtlety and underlying performance of what I gave. That's how motion capture works. It enables anyone to play anything. It's a great tool."

5 /

6 /

"It was really good fun—it was nice to go on a bit of a power trip for a while!"

DOMHNALL GLEESON

GENERAL HUX

Armitage Hux craved power above all. The son of Imperial General Brendol Hux, Armitage didn't hesitate to eliminate his father, consolidating his own power. Raised to the rank of general, Armitage thus became the key man in Snoke's military strategy—and one of the few persons who had direct access to the Supreme Leader. In charge of Starkiller Base, Armitage suggested to Snoke that they test the superweapon embedded in the ice planet, removing the only obstacle in their rise to power: the New Republic. "I can't say enough about Domhnall Gleeson," said director J.J. Abrams, "who was a powerful and wonderfully evil presence in this movie. He played a young General Hux. He had this bloodlust, but also a teacher's pet quality. He brought Hux to life with fervor, power-hungry ugliness. Those kinds of characters are such a cliché. What Domhnall

did was bring this ferocity to it that made you believe he wanted this so badly. He wanted to be a part of the ruling party of the galaxy. You believed it because Domhnall demanded you do."

SUPERWEAPON

Moments before the Starkiller Base superweapon was fired, General Hux addressed the stormtroopers standing in front of him. To Hux, who grew up hearing how the Empire saved the galaxy from the violence of the Clone Wars, this was his chance to make all systems bow to the power of the First Order. "It was a weird scene," commented Gleeson. "We had a big group of extras to look out upon, which was fantastic. And there I was, standing sixty feet above them, wearing a pretty cool coat, screaming about destroying the enemy! It was really good fun—it was nice to go on a bit of a power trip for a while!"

3 / Snoke's immense hologram hides his frail body.

4 / First Order General Armitage Hux.

5 / Senior sculptor Ivan Manzella imagines Supreme Leader Snoke in this paint-over of a photographed sculpt from September 2014.

6 / General Hux addresses the First Order troops.

7 / The chromed stormtrooper (still not Captain Phasma at that time) as imagined by costume concept artist Dermot Power in 2014.

8 / Captain Phasma holding her blaster rifle.

9 / Captain Phasma patrolling a corridor on Starkiller Base.

10 / The First Order fires Starkiller Base's superweapon for the first time.

CAPTAIN PHASMA

Captain Phasma came from the harsh, primitive world of Parnassos. She grew up in a merciless tribe where members had to kill in order to survive. When the First Order subjugated her planet, she joined its troops to escape her cruel existence. Swearing loyalty to its cause, Phasma became an unforgiving commander and a very efficient captain. She led the assault on Jakku to retrieve part of a map to Skywalker's location. When stormtrooper FN-2187 failed to carry out her orders, she didn't suspect he was going to desert and free a Resistance pilot in the process. The two met again, on Starkiller Base, where Finn threatened to shoot her if she didn't disable the base's shields—opening the way for Poe Dameron and his squadron. "Captain Phasma was the captain of the stormtroopers," said actress Gwendoline Christie, who played Phasma. "She was a malevolent force. And she took particular pleasure in her cruelty. It was exciting that something as iconic as *Star Wars* embraced the future, the world's need for gender balance and female empowerment. And it was incredibly thrilling for me to have played that part. I hope it inspired generations of women everywhere to go forward."

CHROMIUM SOLDIER

Phasma's chromium-plated armor was forged from the hull of a Naboo yacht, which was once owned by Emperor Palpatine and later used by General Hux's father. "The design of Phasma came as we were looking for the design for Kylo Ren," recalled Abrams. "We were all stunned at how good it looked. It didn't make sense that he would be wearing this chrome uniform, but there was no way it wasn't going to be in this movie. It was the coolest thing I'd seen. We came up with this idea of a character in charge of the stormtroopers. It was important for me that we had women as well as men in these uniforms. Not that they were just a bunch of male clones. We were lucky to get Gwendoline Christie, who's an incredible actress. Her love of *Star Wars* was so infectious and wonderful."

HAN SOLO & CHEWBACCA

RECLAIMING THE *MILLENNIUM FALCON*

It had been thirty years since the Battle of Endor, and Han Solo and Chewbacca were once again wandering between planets as space smugglers, transporting shipments of questionable cargo and looking for their stolen ship, the *Millennium Falcon*. Their search came to an end when a scavenger, a deserter stormtrooper and a droid brought it back to them.

HAN SOLO

Han gained control of his destiny when he won the *Millennium Falcon* in a game of sabacc—a popular card game. He had been a pirate and a smuggler, but after he met Luke Skywalker and Princess Leia Organa, he joined the Rebel Alliance and helped destroy two different Death Stars. Still, he preferred to introduce himself as a smuggler rather than a war hero. After their son, Ben, turned to the dark side, becoming Kylo Ren, Han and Leia dealt with it by parting ways and going back to what they were good at, smuggling and leading. "It wasn't just about parents who had a difficult kid," said director J.J. Abrams. "It was about these two people who loved each other, who came together, but whose natures were always very different. The idea of Han staying in one place was hard to imagine. The idea that Leia would stop fighting for a cause, and a greater good, was hard to imagine. But they had this kid that was born with equal parts good and evil. He was Darth Vader's grandson, but also Anakin Skywalker's. The idea that it was tumultuous and difficult was one thing, but it's more than just having a bad seed as a kid. The story was what they discovered, and learned along the way: Snoke, who's in charge of the First Order, had targeted their kid." Leia knew there was still light in Ben, and Han tried to save him when he saw him on Starkiller Base, when he attempted to undo what Snoke had done. But Han Solo failed, and then died at the hands of his son.

CHEWBACCA

A Wookiee from the planet Kashyyyk, Chewbacca has been saved by Han Solo on more than one occasion. Teaming with him, Chewbacca later became Han's best friend and copilot. Loyal and brave, he helped the Rebel Alliance restore freedom to the galaxy. Chewie was 234 years old, but Wookiees were long-lived, so he was considered to be in his prime. "When we started working on Chewbacca, we looked back at every photo we could find," recalled Mariak Cork, who supervised the hair department in creature effects. "He looked different in each film, so we had to decide which elements we wanted to pick exactly. In *A New Hope*, there's a definite look we really loved. There's a lot of subtlety, especially in some of the photographs we picked. There was one that was our favorite where he's in the snow, and there's something about that photo, the look of the character, the tone. We tried to copy from that image quite a lot."

They were once again wandering between planets as space smugglers.

3 /

1 / Han Solo and
Chewbacca on
Takodana, outside
Maz Kanata's castle.
(See previous spread)

2 / Chewbacca holding
his handcrafted
bowcaster. (See
previous spread)

3 /Han and Chewie
back on the *Falcon*.

4 / Escaping into
lightspeed with Rey
as copilot.

4 /

"WE'RE HOME"

Han and Chewie opened the giant hangar of the
Eravana, their bulk freighter, to board the ship they
had been seeking for a long time. Their ship, the
Millennium Falcon. Director J. J. Abrams set the stage
for the re-introduction of Han and Chewbacca. "The
audience is pretty sure that our main characters [Finn
and Rey] are doomed. They're surrounded by the First
Order. So the audience expects something terrible to
happen to them. But in that moment of incredible
tension, the door opens, and—it's Han and Chewie! I
had this moment when I was writing on my computer,
and I could literally see the scene of them coming in.
When I wrote, 'Chewie, we're home,' I wasn't sure if
Larry [Kasdan] was going to be like, 'Han wouldn't say
that.' But when he read it, Larry laughed, and thought
it was the right sentiment. It felt like the sort of thing as
a viewer that I wanted to see. I wanted Han Solo to get
back aboard *his* ship, and declare that he was back."

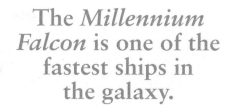

The *Millennium Falcon* is one of the fastest ships in the galaxy.

6 /

WHAT A PIECE OF JUNK!

It may seem like a hunk of junk, but the *Millennium Falcon* was one of the fastest ships in the galaxy. This remarkable Corellian vessel began its life as a YT-1300 light freighter but went through significant remodeling. Its engines doubled in size, its defenses were military-grade destructive weapons, and its velocity and maneuverability were extraordinary. According to Lydia Fry, assistant art director, one of the difficulties regarding the *Falcon* set was that there were no plans of the inside of the ship, so they had to rely on footage and set stills. "There were lots of little quirks within the *Millennium Falcon*," she added. "There were some DVD extras, scenes taken out that showed something you've never seen before. For example, there are certain areas of the ship, like the doorway going into the cockpit. You've seen it from the inside of the cockpit, but you've never seen it from the corridor before. However, you do see it in a deleted scene from *The Empire Strikes Back*, which shows it's relatively plain. But because you've only seen it in a deleted scene on a DVD, we were able to add detail to it."

7 /

5 / Rey flies the *Millennium Falcon* for the first time. The old sensor rectenna, the large dish-shaped sensor and communication array, has been replaced after the original was sheared off.

6 / The *Falcon* lands on Starkiller Base a moment after jumping out of lightspeed in this painting realized by concept artist James Clyne.

7 / The *Falcon* is captured by the giant *Eravana* freighter in this painting realized by concept artist James Clyne.

8 /

A SON

Art director Kevin Jenkins visualized Han Solo as he faced his son on Starkiller Base, calling him Ben, asking him to take off his mask—to come home. Kylo Ren hesitated, but only for a moment. Then he ignited his lightsaber, piercing his father's chest. "The last scene," said actor Harrison Ford, who portrayed Han Solo, "which played out between myself and Kylo Ren, Adam Driver's character, is

obviously of such importance; we all recognized that and felt we had a degree of responsibility. We wanted it to be right. There were deep, powerful feelings involved and there was an effort of investment to guarantee that it was grounded in real, human emotion. As an actor, you can project that with some degree of detail and sophistication. At the same time, it was a raw and powerful moment, yet simple."

8 / Han meets his son Ben Solo on Starkiller Base in this painting realized by art director Kevin Jenkins.

GENERAL LEIA ORGANA

THE RESISTANCE

1 /

Princess Leia Organa of Alderaan had been a key command figure in the Rebel Alliance and one of the greatest opponents of the Empire. Strong-willed and resourceful, she couldn't let the dark side destroy what she fought for. As the First Order rose, she became the leader of the Resistance. With the annihilation of the New Republic, the general became the only hope for the galaxy.

She couldn't let the dark side destroy what she fought for.

3 /

4 /

1 / Resistance leader General Leia Organa, once the princess of Alderaan. (See previous spread)

2 / General Leia on D'Qar, where the Resistance base is located. (See previous spread)

3 /Leia Organa as the leader of the Resistance as imagined by concept artist Glyn Dillon in October 2013.

A WOMAN OF ACTION

Leia was the first one to warn the Senate about the First Order activities. She asked the senators to put a stop to Snoke's arms race, but they ignored her requests, branding her as an alarmist or a warmonger. Educated in martial and political arts, Leia thus decided to form the Resistance—the only movement willing to oppose the First Order. In need of help, she looked for her brother, Luke Skywalker, whom she believed was her only hope to triumph over evil. "I'm an authority figure, I'm an organizer," explained the late actress Carrie Fisher, who played Leia Organa. "Even though I'm Luke's twin, I didn't become a Jedi. I could have been a Jedi. You can't say that without feeling sorry for yourself. Or wistful, and I don't think Leia's wistful. She's authoritative. She's very confident, and that is based on what she has done."

5 /

TOGETHER

The Resistance base was located in the Ileenium system. Leia and the other leaders commanded a small group of brave soldiers and droids united against the vast army of the First Order. Among them was protocol droid C-3PO—who faithfully served his masters, from Anakin to Luke to Leia, during the Clone Wars and the Galactic Civil War. C-3PO was in contact with many droids who served their masters in every corner of the galaxy. Together they formed a network, which could be alerted in case of need. "Princess Leia kept C-3PO, and in some ways he became a slight confidant," explained actor Anthony Daniels, who played fussy protocol droid. "He was a servant, but Leia was always very warm to him, and she understood his difficult side and forgave him. But he was a great companion, so they had each other."

4 / General Leia Organa in the D'Qar base command center.

5 / The Resistance base interior as imagined by concept artist Andrée Wallin.

6 / When Han Solo
and Leia Organa are
reunited, their thoughts
turn to their son Ben,
now the sinister
Kylo Ren.

THE FORCE AWAKENS

MAZ KANATA

ECCENTRIC PIRATE

A collector of countless antiques and treasures, including Skywalker's old lightsaber; Force-sensitive, but not a Jedi; a protector of smugglers and pirates; a traveler who was a thousand years old. This was Maz Kanata, who survived many wars and learned a valuable lesson: although the name may change—the Empire, the Sith, the First Order—there's only one fight, the one against the dark side.

A FRIEND
Looking for some way to get BB-8 to General Leia and the Resistance, Han Solo took Rey, Finn, and the droid to Takodana. He knew Maz Kanata, who lived

there, was their best chance. When she saw him, Maz told Han to go home, to deliver the droid himself. She knew he should stop running away from Leia, from the fight against the First Order and his son. "Maz has known Han Solo since the beginning of his time as a smuggler," said actress Lupita Nyong'o, who played Maz Kanata. "She taught him a lot of what he knows. They had a loving, tough relationship."

> ## She survived many wars and learned a valuable lesson.

They were very fond of each other. Then Han made the mistake of disappearing, which hurt Maz, but she forgave him. Maz did give Han a tough time, though, and challenged him to really step up. He hadn't seen Leia in a long time... and Maz reminded Han that he had to face his past. To face his demons."

THE CASTLE

Her castle, built near a lake and a primordial forest, welcomed travelers of every type: criminals, gamblers, government emissaries, headhunters, and spies. To many, it was the last bastion of civilization in the Outer Rim—the frontier region of the galaxy before the Unknown Regions. "It was the center of, not only the film, but the center of the story," explained

3 /

4 /

6 /

set decorator Lee Sandales. "A lot of things were revealed here. Everything about *The Force Awakens* happened here, at Maz's castle. It was the one set that took me a long time to get into my head. First of all, the concept of a *Star Wars* castle. It was really difficult to actually achieve that. Because it wasn't just a castle—it was a place where every kind of being from the galaxy would come to. It was kind of a home for pirates. Some of them were pretty shady characters. I had a lot of fun with it. The inspiration

came from a Ralph McQuarrie drawing of a single lamp. And, from there, I was able to develop the whole world of all the dressings, all the fixtures, all the fittings, all the furniture, all the fabrics."

MOTION-CAPTURE ACTRESS

Like Snoke, played by actor Andy Serkis, Maz Kanata was a CGI character, and the scenes in which she appeared were shot in motion capture, as Nyong'o recalled: "A typical day on the set involved

5 /

getting into makeup. Actually, it was dots! Every morning, they would put a hundred and forty-nine dots on my face. The whole process took between forty-five minutes to an hour. I then put on a gray suit that had triangles, which looked like road signs, velcroed all over it. They were everywhere. After that, I put on kneepads and restraints to help with my mobility. Lastly, they put a headcam on me, with four cameras to capture every movement my face made. Then, we began."

THE SKYWALKER SAGA CONTINUES

THE LAST JEDI

LUKE SKYWALKER

JEDI SURVIVOR

1 /

Luke Skywalker was living a simple life, far from his twin sister, Leia Organa, who desperately needed his help to fight the First Order, and far from his failure, Ben Solo, who had turned to the dark side. When the *Millennium Falcon* appeared on the horizon, and the past came calling on him in the form of his lightsaber, Luke refused. For he desired to put an end to the Jedi once and for all.

HIS FAILURE

It should have been the beginning of a new era for the Jedi—that is what Luke Skywalker saw in his future after the death of his father, Anakin Skywalker. He wanted to pass on what he had learned, but he had to discover more about the history of the Jedi and their teachings first. For years he traveled across the galaxy, following any trace of Jedi lore to reconstruct a fragmented past—a past almost completely removed during the Imperial era. At the end of this quest,

Luke desired to put an end to the Jedi.

Skywalker revived the Jedi Order and started a training temple. But when he saw the vast darkness in his apprentice Ben Solo, the powerful son of Han Solo and Leia, and how Snoke had corrupted him, Luke hesitated. For a moment, he even imagined killing him. The moment passed, but everything was lost. Ben became Kylo Ren, destroyed the temple, and slaughtered most of the students. The balance between the light and the dark was broken. Holding himself responsible for the tragedy, hoping to bury the past and the Jedi along with it, Luke vanished. As the destination for his exile, he chose an island that had a strong connection with the Force—where the order was founded, and the first Jedi temple erected a long time before. It took him years to locate it. "The

THE ISLAND

Rey found Luke on the planet Ahch-To—a place she had already seen in her visions on Jakku. Hidden in a long-forgotten region of the galaxy, Ahch-To was a harsh planet orbiting two suns. Mostly covered in water, lacking any city or form of technology, it was beaten by cold winds and violent storms. Ireland offered the perfect setting the production was looking for. "I wanted something that looked like the Skellig islands," recalls production designer Rick Heinrichs, "so we started on the west coast of Ireland, and we managed to find something within eyesight of Skellig. We needed dramatic cliffs with a certain view of the sun, so we could capture the precarious environment and beauty of the set. I think the first time Rian saw our location, it clicked with him right away." On Ahch-To, Luke led a life not too dissimilar from the one he used to lead on Tatooine in his youth: He harvested everything he needed, caught fish with a spear, and sheltered from the island's unpredictable weather inside his ancient, stacked-stone hut, in a village abandoned a long time ago. The village set was shot in two different locations: At Pinewood Studios, England, where every aspect of shooting could take place in a controlled environment; and in Ireland, where the same set was shipped and rebuilt to take advantage of the natural environment and ambiance.

6 /

4 / Inside the massive husk of a tree trunk, which the first Jedi used as a library, Luke keeps the original Jedi texts, containing the history and secrets of the Jedi Order. As production designer Rick Heinrichs explained, "This tree is on this completely treeless island, in a protected fold in the side of the mountain. And it was kind of hollowed out—you weren't sure if it was done by nature, or by the Jedi craftsmen."

5 / Concept artist Mauro Borrelli visualizes the tree, whose shape was modeled on the Rebel Alliance logo.

6 / Luke Skywalker wearing his work clothes, as imagined by costume concept artist Jock.

A MASTER NO MORE

When Rey handed Luke his old lightsaber, the weapon built by his father, he rejected it. And when she asked him to help her and the Resistance, to come fight with them, he refused. To him, the Jedi needed to end. Stubborn and tenacious, Rey didn't give up. The stakes were too high. And finally, with a little help from Luke's old astromech droid, R2-D2, she persuaded the aging master to teach her the ways of the Force. Luke just wanted her to understand his reasons, then leave. But Rey proved to be different from anyone else he had ever trained. "She was basically trying to convince Luke to leave with her," said actress Daisy Ridley, who played Rey, "to go back to the Resistance. And Luke was totally hard on her. Pretty harsh, actually." But Rey persisted. Even on Jakku, in the backend of nowhere in space, she'd heard stories about Luke. And he made Rey realize that the stories weren't all that they seemed to be, that good people make bad choices—and bad people make good choices, too."

9 /

7 / Luke holds his lightsaber for the first time in decades.

8 / As Luke hesitates, Yoda, just a Force ghost, destroys the Jedi library with a bolt of lightning.

9 / Chewbacca helped Rey get to Ahch-To and is ready to help her get the attention of his old friend, Luke Skywalker.

SO LONG, HAN

Luke Skywalker had closed himself off to the Force. He cut off all connection to the energy field, isolating himself. He could not sense his friends or his sister—and no one could sense him. So he didn't know about Han's death until Rey and Chewbacca told him. "We shot in Ireland," recalled actor Joonas Suotamo, who played Chewbacca in the film. "The scenery was breathtaking. We filmed in a beautiful village on a cliff top. That was the first time I got to work with Mark [Hamill]. To be there with him portraying Luke Skywalker yet again was very exhilarating for me. I got to bring my dad on set that day! I was so happy he got to see what I saw. My dad was the one who showed me *Star Wars* for the first time. I grew up loving the characters. I even wanted to be Luke, because my hair was blond when I was very young! It was a big honor to have that scene with Mark and Daisy atop the cliff."

YODA

"Failure most of all. The greatest teacher, failure is," said Yoda, who appeared as a Force ghost on Ahch-To to help Luke destroy the Jedi library and the text preserved inside. Though Yoda died on Dagobah years before, he was able to communicate with Luke, providing him with invaluable advice. Yoda was a practical character controlled by puppeteers Frank Oz, Brian Herring, and Dave Chapman. "Yoda was like

Chewie and other characters: they were untouchable," explained Neil Scanlan, creative supervisor for creature effects and special makeup effects. "You cannot and should not modify them in any way, shape, or form. Yoda became a little like Chewie because we had to go back and look at what Stuart [Freeborn, the makeup artist who designed Yoda for *The Empire Strikes Back*] had done, and how Stuart made him. It was a fantastic road of discovery. One of the greatest things we found was the original mold of Yoda, located in the Lucasfilm Archive. We made a new cast from that mold. Through that process, and by looking at archival pictures and talking to some of the people involved in previous films, we were able to replicate the Yoda puppet. It was the closest replica of the original that one could have."

THE LAST FIGHT

All hope was lost. The surviving members of the Resistance were trapped inside an abandoned rebel base on the planet Crait. A distress signal had been broadcast to all their allies, but no response was received. Then Luke Skywalker appeared inside the base, comforted General Leia, and stepped out, ready to face Kylo Ren for the first and last time. "The confrontation between Luke and Kylo is the ultimate set-piece and standoff, and I think it was quite unexpected," said visual effects supervisor Ben Morris. "Their face-off occurred on a terrain of complete devastation, among exploded elements of TIE fighters and ski speeders." It also took place on top of a vivid, blood-red battleground. As Morris noted, "We've got a flat, white plain, which is covered in crystal dust. But underneath that, you've got this incredibly rich red crystal structure that gets kicked up by the vehicles... You see the surface go from beautiful and pristine to almost like a blood bath." It's here that Kylo commands the First Order to unleash a lethal barrage on Luke, who miraculously steps out of the cloud of red, seemingly unharmed. We built a small set piece on a stage, and all the action involved Mark and Adam." ☻

THE LAST JEDI

REY &
KYLO REN

A REVEALING CONNECTION

Rey's abilities could easily have led her to the dark side, ruled by anger, fear, and aggression. Rey needed to find someone to guide her along the right path. But while she found a master in Luke Skywalker on Ahch-To island, Rey also experienced a mysterious, intense Force connection with Kylo Ren, her enemy—a connection whose nature and meaning changed everything.

3 /

> ## "Rey had this desire to connect with her past, and she had some notion that she might find answers on Ahch-To."
> RIAN JOHNSON

1 / Rey holding Luke's lightsaber during the fight aboard Supreme Leader Snoke's Mega-Destroyer, the *Supremacy* Rey patiently waits in front of Luke's hut on Ahch-To. (See previous spread)

2 / After destroying his mask Kylo Ren shows his face to his enemies. (See previous spread)

3 / Rey patiently waits in front of Luke's hut on Ahch-To.

REY OF LIGHT

The more time Rey spent on the island—training with Luke Skywalker, learning about the Jedi past and the failures of the Jedi Order, learning about the fine line between the light and the dark side of the Force—the more she realized that something was calling her. And she was afraid. As director Rian Johnson explained: "Rey had this desire to connect with her past, and she had some notion that she might find answers on Ahch-To. Not just about who her parents are or where she

comes from, but wanting to know what her place is in all of this. When she arrives on that island, there's a part of Rey—and a big part of us—that expects she will get that information from Luke." But it's not the old Jedi Master who gives Rey the answers which she's looking for. Some answers, like what happened between Luke and Ben Solo and how Skywalker's training temple was destroyed, came from a strange connection with Kylo Ren. The relationship Rey had with Kylo and with the dark side was something Luke had never seen before.

4 / The Force connection between Rey and Kylo, and the duality of light and dark they represent, is visualized in this painting by VFX art director James Clyne.

5 / Kylo prepares to hand Luke's lightsaber to Supreme Leader Snoke.

The dark side fueled Kylo's ambition, driving him to desire more.

5 /

KYLO THE DARK

His training should have been completed. Kylo Ren killed his father and proved to Supreme Leader Snoke that he was worthy of becoming the dark lord his master wanted him to be. But the words of his father echoed in his mind. Han Solo said Snoke was only using Kylo for his power. The dark side fueled Kylo's ambition, driving him to desire more, to plan on assuming the mantle of power he thought he deserved. But before that, he had to understand why the Force was binding him and the scavenger from Jakku together. "Kylo Ren was the character who I was the most excited to explore when I was writing," recalled Johnson. "In the first *Star Wars* films, Vader was a great villain, but he was never someone who you identified with. You identified with Luke's relationship to him. Vader was the monster. And then he was the scary father, and then he was the father you had to reconcile with. Kylo is not really that for Rey. It's almost like Rey and Kylo are two halves of the same protagonist. Rey the light and Kylo the dark. Kylo represents the anger of adolescence and wanting to reject your parents, and wanting to break away, which I think, to some extent, all of us can identify with, as much as we can identify with the hopeful Rey looking up at the stars from her planet. That's my favorite kind of 'bad guy'—the ones that you can identify with."

6 / A medical droid takes care of Kylo's scar, inflicted by Rey on Starkiller Base, in this art by concept artist Roberto Fernández Castro.

7 / Fernández Castro's art is realized on screen.

8 / According to sound designer Ren Klyce, director Rian Johnson didn't use any visual effect to connect Rey and Kylo. He did it all on camera, with simple cuts. The sound was essential for the success of the process: "All the Force connections have a sort of different architecture to them in terms of the construction of their sounds, but they do have one thing in common. I used [sound] samples of ocean kelp and microphones under the ice to create these very strange, undulating, organic sounds that don't feel synthetic but feel odd. And then when all those sounds vanish is when they Force connect."

NEVER ALONE

When Luke discovered the Force connection between Rey and Kylo, he immediately stopped it, destroying Rey's hut with the Force and demanding that she leave the island immediately. He believed there was too much dark in Kylo Ren, that he couldn't be saved or redeemed. But Rey had seen Kylo's future and knew that Luke was wrong. The connection between them was out of their control but gave both Kylo and Rey the awareness they were not alone. Their fates were intertwined. Daisy Ridley, the actress who portrayed Rey, explained a bit more about the Force connection between the two. "Even though they were in two separate environments, the characters were connected. Through that connection, they built this intimacy. Rey and Kylo both opened up to each other, more than they had to anyone else before." When asked if Rey tried to influence Kylo, Ridley said, "I never felt like I was persuading him. But neither character was trying to do anything to the other, really. They were just having a conversation. All they did was open up to each other. Kylo shared reasons behind the decisions he had made. There wasn't any attempt to convince on anyone's part."

7

9 /

9 / Later in the film, Rey and Kylo Ren find themselves aboard Snoke's ship, surrounded by the eight members of Snoke's Praetorian Guard.

10 / Accepting her destiny, trusting in the Force as Luke taught her, Rey removes the boulders that trap the Resistance survivors on Crait. Art by concept artists Kim Frederiksen and James Carson.

11 / Adam Driver (Kylo Ren) on set, rehearsing the fight scene with the Praetorian Guard and the stunt team.

10 /

INTO THE CAVE

The most essential teaching Rey received from Luke was about the nature of the Force. When he asked her to close her eyes and breathe, to reach out with her feelings, she started to see things: the island, life, death, and decay that feeds life. She felt warmth, cold, peace, and violence; and among all of it a balance, an energy. Inside herself, Rey had the same energy, the same Force. It didn't belong to the Jedi, Luke explained, and it wouldn't end if the Jedi died. Rey understood, but she also felt something else: a gloomy sea cave on the other side of Ahch-To and the dark side calling her, offering to give her answers to all the questions that had troubled her to this point. Who was she? Who were her parents? What was her role in the conflict between the First Order and the Resistance? Without hesitation, Rey went straight into that cave and discovered the only answer that mattered was herself. Realizing this revelation on screen was a visual challenge for everyone, as visual effects supervisor Ben Morris explained: "We didn't want to do a typical video effect. And so, we spent a lot of time with design supervisor Kevin Jenkins and his art department. The key thing for us was we didn't want to shoot all the different mirror versions of Rey separately. We wanted exactly the same performance and instance of Daisy as she appeared within the mirror to be shot at the same time. And so we set up a whole series of cameras that were all synchronized to film at the same time, and they were all at the perfect perspective for that shot to show her movements. That allowed us to change the phase of her performance." ☯

The only answer that mattered was herself.

12 / The Praetorian Guard is defeated. Snoke is dead. "It's time to let old things die," Kylo tells Rey. "Snoke, Skywalker. The Sith, the Jedi, the rebels...let it all die. Rey. I want you to join me. We can rule together and bring a new order to the galaxy." He proves to Rey that to him she isn't nothing. But she can't join him; she can't betray the Resistance and General Leia. Using the Force, the two battle for Skywalker's lightsaber, which explodes and breaks into pieces.

13 / Rian Johnson and Daisy Ridley with the crew on set, shooting the cave scene.

THE FIRST ORDER

FOLLOWING THE LEADER

It may have lost the destructive power of Starkiller Base, but with the New Republic in shambles, the First Order continued to spread its evil like a plague across the entire galaxy. Under the leadership of Supreme Leader Snoke, General Hux and Kylo Ren organized a massive strike against the Resistance. And new, devastating technology would make the escape of General Leia's fleet impossible.

UNKNOWN POWER

Supreme Leader Snoke was disappointed by his young, faithful apprentice. Luke Skywalker, the seed of the Jedi Order, lived. The Resistance lived. And Rey, a scavenger no one had ever heard about, was able to defeat Ren in a lightsaber fight. Taunting Kylo Ren, calling him "young Solo," Snoke tried to

> The First Order continued to spread its evil like a plague across the entire galaxy.

destabilize his mind to keep him and his exceptional abilities under control. As director Rian Johnson explained: "[Snoke] was a very powerful villain. He was like the Emperor in the original trilogy. He was like the source of evil behind [Kylo Ren]." The character was once again played by actor Andy Serkis, who first brought life to Snoke in *The Force Awakens*. "It was my first time working with Andy,"

"He was like the Emperor in the original trilogy."

RIAN JOHNSON

continued Johnson, "and it was my first time really working with a motion-capture character. Snoke was entirely CG, and was built from Andy's mo-cap performance. Andy was extraordinary. Just seeing him perform, we were mesmerized. It was incredible to see what ILM [Industrial Light & Magic] did, to see how they captured Andy's performance in this animated character. It was magical." In the previous film, Snoke only appeared as a giant hologram. This was the first time the audience saw him in person, sharing the privilege with Kylo Ren and General Hux. Visual effects supervisor Ben Morris said that bringing him back down to a real physical entity was an incredible challenge. Janet Lewin, vice president of visual effects, agreed: "The character design had to stay true to what audiences saw in *The Force Awakens*, but we wanted to ground him in reality, because it was Rian's desire to make him a real human battling Kylo and Rey. To make him a little more human, we actually changed some of the asymmetries of his face. As a hologram, his design was very extreme and it was hard for the audience to connect to him because he was so massive."

CUT IN HALF

When Rey was brought before Snoke in his enormous throne room aboard the *Supremacy*—a *Mega*-class Star Destroyer—the First Order leader immediately became aware of her astonishing power. The mysterious scavenger posed a real threat to all of them and had to be executed. But Kylo Ren betrayed Snoke, disobeying his direct order, and used the Force to ignite Skywalker's lightsaber (which sat on the arm of Snoke's throne), slicing the Supreme Leader in half. "Snoke was kind of like this last stand-in father figure," said Adam Driver. The Kylo Ren actor felt the scene was particularly significant. "It wasn't a moment of rejoicing," the actor said about the killing of Snoke. "It's not like Kylo was suddenly free of his past. It's more complicated than that. He basically finds himself in a new situation where he has everything he might have ever wanted, but now he has no one to share it with." After a furious battle against Snoke's Praetorian Guard, Rey left the *Supremacy*, and Kylo Ren proclaimed himself the new Supreme Leader of the First Order. General Hux, cowed by the power of the dark side, could only acknowledge Kylo's ascendancy.

1 / Supreme Leader Snoke in his throne room aboard the *Supremacy*.

2 / According to costume designer Michael Kaplan, director Rian Johnson loved the idea of using gold for Snoke. "I said, 'What if he was gold?' And I showed him the kind of gold I was thinking of, and what it would look like. Rian was very happy with it. I also had to look at the bigger picture, because we had this huge set with a lot of red and black in it. I thought gold would be extraordinary, something that wasn't being used at all on the set. So it would stand out and be a strong presence."

2 /

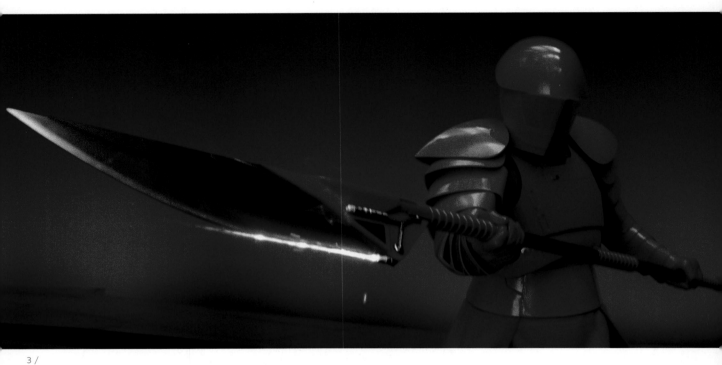

3 /

PRAETORIAN GUARD

Supreme Leader Snoke's elite warriors had no identity, and no one knew their origins. They stood motionless in the throne room, taking action only when the Supreme Leader was endangered. Implacable, loyal, and ever-vigilant, they protected Snoke from whoever represented a threat, including his guests, generals, and his apprentice, Kylo Ren.

When activated, their layered red armor created an intense local magnetic field that deflected blaster fire and even glancing lightsaber blows. Their tempered metal blades were made even more lethal by a high-frequency vibration created across the cutting edge by a compact ultrasonic generator. Moreover, the energized blade parallel to each cutting edge could parry a lightsaber.

3 / One of Snoke's Praetorian Guard, ready to avenge the death of the Supreme Leader.

4 /

5 /

> ## "Hux had his eye on the throne, and Kylo was a challenge to that."
>
> DOMHNALL GLEESON

SECOND-IN-COMMAND

General Armitage Hux was aware that even with the destruction of Starkiller Base, no underground movement, no planet, no system could match the military might of the First Order. Not just for its vast armada or the near limitless number of troops it could deploy, but for the new weapon his engineers had developed starting from a theory conceived in the Imperial era: active hyperspace tracking. With the ability to track Resistance ships through hyperspace, Hux knew it was only a matter of time before they could put an end to their last opponent and finally rule the galaxy. "I think Hux occupied a strange territory in that he's not in between Snoke and Kylo," said actor Domhnall Gleeson, who played Armitage Hux. "First came Snoke, then Kylo, and then Hux. Each operated different arms of the First Order and had different powers. They were good at different things. There was a wildness about Kylo that we saw in *The Force Awakens* that Hux didn't have. Hux was more disciplined and ruthless. I thought Hux had his eye on the throne, and Kylo was a challenge to that. Hux was also scared of Kylo, and hated him—but respected him in a strange way, because Kylo was so powerful. So I think all those things were in the mix. Ultimately, power was all Hux really cared about."

4 / There are four pairs of sentinels in the Praetorian Guard, and each pair wields the same weapons— high-tech versions of ancient analog weapons from across the galaxy: an electro-bisento, a vibro-voulge, a bilari electro-chain whip, and the twin vibro-arbir blades.

5 / General Armitage Hux on the bridge of a First Order Star Destroyer.

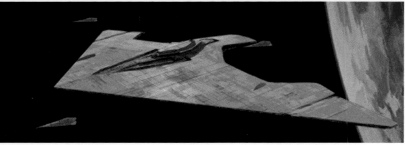

CRUSHING ANY OPPOSITION

The loss of Starkiller Base at the hands of the Resistance fighters didn't lead to a significant setback for the forces of evil. In fact, Supreme Leader Snoke's organization had never had a central base on a planet that served as the capital. Instead, its officers and troops operated aboard myriad crafts, constantly moving throughout the galaxy. Their enormous fleet of Star Destroyers, Dreadnoughts, and TIE fighters, their AT-M6 walkers, and their stormtroopers were all they needed to seize military control of the galaxy. Snoke himself commanded the *Supremacy*, the only *Mega*-class Star Destroyer ever built. Millions of officers, technicians, droids, and stormtroopers served aboard it, loyally carrying out the Supreme Leader's orders. Dwarfing the First Order's own immense Star Destroyers, this colossal weapon of war was capable of wiping out the entire Resistance fleet. As visual effects supervisor Ben Morris explained, its design represented an evolution from the previous film: "The First Order ships were always long and thin and pointy. We wanted to come up with a new design for the *Supremacy*, so we created this large wing shape that worked. When the camera moved over the ship, there was this fairly ominous quality. It was almost like some huge manta ray coming over you. The size of the other Star Destroyers was insignificant in comparison. They were like smaller fish traveling along with the manta ray." ☻

FINN & ROSE

MORE THAN A TROOPER

1 /

2 /

F inn was a hero—or at least, that's what everyone in the Resistance fleet thought. But he didn't feel like one. The only thing Finn cared about was finding Rey. But fate and Rose Tico took him on a daring mission to save the Resistance. Ultimately, Finn would prove himself to be the hero the galaxy needed, one who knew right from wrong and refused to run away when he had the chance.

RUNAWAY

Severely injured by Kylo Ren on Starkiller Base, Finn was evacuated on the *Millennium Falcon* then brought aboard the Resistance flagship, the *Raddus*, where doctors put him into an emergency bacta suit to recover. Unconscious the whole time, Finn thought he was still on Starkiller Base when he woke up. He was not aware that Rey reached Ahch-To to become a Jedi, or that the Resistance fleet was being chased across the galaxy by the First Order, which was getting closer and closer. Nor did he know that

The only thing Finn cared about was finding Rey.

everyone had heard his story, how he left the First Order (the only stormtrooper known to have defected) and helped destroy Starkiller Base. They believed him to be a hero who wouldn't flee in the face of danger. But Finn wasn't quite so sure. He only wanted to find Rey and keep her safe. "Finn had evolved from *The Force Awakens*," said actor John Boyega. "He was more aware of his part in this story. He was more affected by the events that happened before, and brought that same energy and struggle into *The Last Jedi*. But, at the same time, he was still confused about where he belonged. Although he had matured, became more of a fighter, there were still some loose ends in terms of his character development."

4

"Finn was more aware of his part in this story."

JOHN BOYEGA

FINN

As he attempted to leave the *Raddus* to find Rey, Finn ran into Rose Tico, a maintenance worker. She recognized him as "*the* Finn," one of the most famous Resistance heroes. Meeting Rose changed everything for him, as Boyega explained: "Finn didn't ask to be a superhero and with that kind of reputation, but he had to live up to it now since people believed in him." Together, the two came up with a daring plan to help the Resistance fleet escape the First Order. Once again, Finn was about to risk his life for the right cause—something only a hero would do. "[Rose] was helping Finn understand that, in the bigger picture, it wasn't just about him," said producer Ram Bergman. "[She] was a true believer in the Resistance and she was kind of idealistic, but she was also very practical. She was the one who really believed in the cause, and she was going to be the angel on Finn's shoulder."

1 / A bacta suit (early design) helps Finn recover from Kylo's direct blow, in this painting by concept artist Chris Weston. (See previous spread)

2 / Despite what he thinks of himself, Finn is not a coward and is ready to sacrifice himself for the Resistance. (See previous spread)

3 / Rose and Finn arguing about what they should do in the casino in Canto Bight. (See previous spread)

4 / Rose and Finn leave Cantonica aboard the luxury yacht *Libertine*.

5 / Actor John Boyega and director Rian Johnson on set.

7 /

8 /

"Rose had always been the one behind pipes, fixing things."

KELLY MARIE TRAN

TICO SISTERS

Rose Tico and her older sister, Paige, were raised by their parents Hue and Thanya in the Otomok system, in the peaceful mining colony of Hays Minor. They grew up dreaming of leaving their home and traveling the galaxy to see its countless marvels... until the First Order arrived. Unbeknownst to the New Republic, the evil military organization began razing the cities of Otomok to test its armaments. It stole their children for recruitment and left the survivors nothing to live for—except their hate. Wearing twin medallions with the symbol of the Otomok system, Paige and Rose joined the Resistance cause—the former serving as a ventral gunner aboard a bomber, the latter as a member of the support crew. "[Paige] was so cool," said actress Kelly Tran, who played Rose Tico. "Not only was she a gunner, she was

someone who people would essentially think of as a hero. Rose was kind of the opposite of that. She worked in maintenance—she was a nobody. And her sister was always the cool one, the one out there at the forefront of the action. Rose had always been the one behind pipes, fixing things. And something happened at the beginning of the movie that pulled Rose into the journey. She met Finn, and they went on a series of crazy adventures together. It was really interesting to see how their relationship evolved throughout the movie." Paige Tico died during the evacuation of the Resistance base on D'Qar. The Cobalt and Crimson squadrons of heavy bombers helped cover the evacuation, and succeeded, but they were all destroyed by the First Order armada. Paige was serving aboard the *Cobalt Hammer*, sitting inside the armored rotating turret suspended beneath the bomb rack.

6 / Rose as played by Kelly Marie Tran.

7 / Paige Tico aboard a Resistance bomber.

8 / Rose's medallion, with the symbol of the Otomok system, representing Hays Minor.

9 /

9 / Actress Veronica Ngo (Paige Tico) on set, shooting a scene aboard the Cobalt Hammer bomber.

10 / BB-8 accompanies Finn and Rose on their sabotage mission aboard the enemy's flagship and saves them by commandeering an AT-ST walker. Art by James Clyne.

10 /

REMNANTS OF THE CIVIL WAR

The MG-100 StarFortresses were the Resistance's heavy bombers. From their modular bombing magazines, they could drop more than one thousand proton bombs, which were magnetically drawn to their targets. "We were pretty far into the development of the bomber, and I felt like we had knocked out the big request from Rian [Johnson] in terms of their layout. It felt very rebel, very Resistance, very *Star Wars*. But one of Rian's big notes was, 'Make it more bovine.' And I was like, 'What? What does that mean? A bovine?' I think I even had to look it up! Essentially, he wanted a less aggressive look, something more heavy and armored, more cowlike. As designers, we tend to want to make things cool. But sometimes that doesn't go along with what the story is trying to say. So we softened the edges, made it more primitive, and the bomber found its look. It took me weeks to understand what Rian wanted when he said, 'Make it more bovine.' But I think the final product shows it."

REBEL SCUM

Aboard the *Supremacy*, Finn fought against Captain Phasma, his former superior in the First Order army. She considered Finn to be a deserter, and wanted him to pay the price for his treachery. "The Finn and Phasma relationship started to become a thing," said Boyega. "I originally thought, *Okay, we were on two separate paths. She wasn't looking for me, and I wasn't looking for her.* Then Finn and Phasma ended up face to face, which resulted in a major fight between the two. And it was a brutal fight that showed Finn's skills and original stormtrooper training, where there's no room for fear. And it also showed how strong and resourceful Phasma was." Using the ax of an executioner stormtrooper, Finn was able to smash Phasma's chromed helmet, revealing her face for the first

"It was exciting to keep that sense of mystery."

GWENDOLINE CHRISTIE

time. "There were conversations of how much would be revealed," recalled actress Gwendoline Christie, who played Phasma. "It ranged from a large to small proportion. I think it was exciting to keep that sense of mystery. We were still divining who Phasma was, and what motivated her. So [costume designer] Michael Kaplan and the whole creative team decided to just reveal one eye. There was something very nice about the slow unveiling of this person, and who she was." ☾

11 / Captain Phasma's face is revealed, as visualized by concept artist Tonči Zonjić.

12 / Actress Gwendoline Christie on set, wearing Phasma's armor. "It was so shiny," commented Christie, "that other members of the cast and crew came and fixed their hair in the suit because it was like a mirror."

THE GENERAL

AND THE LAST REBELS

2 /

I t was the most desperate hour for General Leia Organa and her allies. Down to four main ships, chased by the merciless First Order fleet and a dangerous new technology that could track them through hyperspace, the Resistance teetered on the brink of destruction. But Luke Skywalker's twin sister wouldn't succumb to despair. All the members of the Resistance looked up to her, to the princess who once defeated an Empire, as a symbol of hope.

FOR THE FUTURE

It was only a matter of time before the Resistance ships would be destroyed by the First Order, one by one. General Leia, who had lost many friends and loved ones in the war against the First Order, feared

It was the most desperate hour for General Leia Organa and her allies.

she could no longer carry on. But as her friend Vice Admiral Holdo reminded her, she could, she must, and she would. The Resistance needed her tenacity and determination to show them the way. Then Kylo Ren, aboard his prototype TIE silencer, led an attack on the Resistance flagship, the *Raddus*. His torpedoes destroyed the hangar bay, but he was unable to open

3 /

5 /

> ## "She used the Force, which we had never really seen her do."
>
> BEN MORRIS

fire on the bridge where his mother was. A moment later, one of the Special Forces fighter pilots took that decision from him. The bridge exploded and many died, lost in the vacuum of space. The Force allowed Leia to survive, but she fell unconscious. "It was always in the original script, that the audience would witness Leia being sucked out into the vacuum of space," said visual effects supervisor Ben Morris about this scene. "Has she made it? Have we lost her? We wanted to be very careful with how we played that moment. There was a lot of conversation about the

4 /

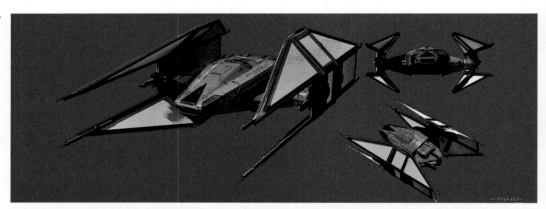

1 / Leia is ready to fight once again when the Resistance forces are trapped in a former rebel base on Crait. (See previous spread)

2 / C-3PO is never too far from Leia, whom he's known since she was the princess of Alderaan. (See previous spread)

3 / The late Carrie Fisher (General Leia Organa) on set, ready to save the galaxy once again.

4 / Different versions of Kylo Ren's TIE silencer. Art by James Clyne.

5 / General Leia
demotes Poe Dameron
after his decision
resulted in the loss
of all the Resistance
bombers.

6 / Poe Dameron
wearing his flight suit
with the Rebel
Alliance logo.

moment when Leia was outside in space, about how
we could portray something that needed to feel real.
But it was also a hugely significant moment—when
Leia defies what you thought was her death. She used
the Force, which we had never really seen her do in
the other films. We wanted to work out a very delicate
and beautiful way of showing Leia in space as she
starts to use the Force." Leia's apparent loss was a
boon to the First Order, but the Resistance would not
be so easily shaken. The general had prepared a new
generation of heroes who would take her place and
allow hope to survive.

A NEW LEADER

When the First Order fleet caught the Resistance in the
middle of the evacuation of D'Qar, Poe Dameron
didn't hesitate. Following his instincts, he approached
the enemy's Dreadnought alone aboard his starfighter
and took out all its cannons before anyone realized
that he was just a decoy. Thanks to him, the Resistance
bombers could start their attack, buying time for the
evacuation to be completed. But Poe's recklessness
took over. When General Leia ordered him to
disengage, Poe switched off his communications. He
wanted the bombers to take down the Dreadnought.
And they did, but the cost was too high. For his
disregard of a direct order, Leia demoted him. She
knew that Poe represented the future of the Resistance,
but he had to learn a lesson: He couldn't solve
everything by jumping in his X-wing and blowing
something up. He must learn patience and strategy. He
must think like a leader. "The theme of mentors ran
through this whole series," explained director Rian
Johnson. "To me, it made a lot of sense that Leia would
be a mentor to Poe. If Leia was the general in charge of
the Resistance, her ace pilot was Poe. He's a great *Star
Wars* character in *The Force Awakens*, there wasn't a
ton of conflict. You knew who he was, because he was
an awesome pilot. And that was perfect. And you loved
him from the get-go. But I wanted to push him a little
more, and put him in a tough spot."

6 /

"Holdo was, in fact, mercurial—you weren't sure what you were going to get."

LAURA DERN

VICE ADMIRAL HOLDO

There were few people General Organa trusted more than Amilyn Holdo. She was born on Gatalenta, whose inhabitants were known for their poetry, peacefulness, and compassion. While still in their teens, Leia and Holdo served together in the Imperial Senate, and the two become quick friends, each sensing a kindred spirit in the other. Eventually, they became members of the Rebel Alliance right from the beginning—so joining the Resistance came naturally. When Leia was injured, Holdo was chosen to take her place. Firm and brave, Holdo was aware that the Resistance was the last spark of hope left in the galaxy and that they must survive at all costs. But many, made insecure by Leia's absence, didn't trust Holdo and wanted to know if she had a real plan to save the Resistance. "You didn't know who she was," said actress Laura Dern, who played Holdo. "You knew she was trained by Leia, but Holdo was, in fact, mercurial—you weren't sure what you were going to get. As the story unfolded, the people around Holdo began to question her more and more. It was an incredibly good time, because Rian, Kathy Kennedy, and Ram [Bergman] cared deeply about how their characters were represented. In this case, they cared how a woman was represented in a place of power. It was important to Rian that Holdo had room to be very ethereal and otherworldly, even spiritual. She wasn't going to dress like a man and show up in military gear to save the day. It was an interesting choice and something we haven't seen in films."

10 /

TRAPPED ON CRAIT

While the last fighters of the Resistance retreated to an old Rebel Alliance base on the remote world Crait, Holdo stayed behind aboard the *Raddus*. She activated the hyperdrive and jumped through the *Supremacy* at lightspeed. Her sacrifice saved many lives, but on Crait, the fight wasn't over yet. A desolate, moonless world, Crait was covered in barren salt flats, a thick crust of vibrant red crystals beneath them. A mining company first discovered the planet, but its facilities were soon abandoned. The rebel engineers then used those facilities to start the construction of a heavily armored base. They never finished, because the Empire became aware of the base's location. The rebels fled Crait, leaving behind artillery emplacements as well as transports, equipment, weapons, and speeders. Everything was old, rusty, and barely functional. The Resistance fighters had no choice but to make the most of it. Johnson said that he had a precise visual idea from

12 /

13 /

11 / The *Raddus*, piloted by Holdo, tears the *Supremacy* in half at lightspeed.

12 / General Leia, Poe Dameron, C-3PO, and other surviving members of the Resistance leave the *Raddus* and Vice Admiral Holdo to their destiny.

the very start of what Crait might be like. "It would be white, with a thin layer of salt, like topsoil," Johnson said. "And then under that would be this ruby-red sort of crystal foundation." As visual effects supervisor Ben Morris explained, the design of Crait was inspired by real salt flats: "We had the wonderful opportunity to travel to Bolivia to the high Altiplano salt plains. We shot a lot of visual reference for the skies and for the structures of natural salt that occurs there. And that fit into the look of the entire sequence."

LIKE OLD TIMES

When Luke Skywalker suddenly arrived inside the Resistance base on Crait, Leia knew he was there to meet her son, Ben Solo, in a duel. She also felt that Ben couldn't be saved, that her son was gone. But her brother replied that no one's ever really gone. "I felt really good about that scene," said Carrie Fisher. "It was very emotional—for me and for Mark. That hadn't happened to me as an actor before. I cried. We hadn't seen each other for a long time. It was the

15 /

13 / Poe Dameron
and a handful of
brave pilots fly the
V-4X-D ski speeders
against the upgraded,
terrifying First Order
MegaCalibur Six
walkers. Built upon
a civilian sporting
vehicle, the V-4X-D
"was not very good
at flying, it was a bit
rubbish, and it was
very unstable. It was
falling apart around
them." explained
design supervisor
Kevin Jenkins.

14 / Vulptex early
studies, backlit
version as imagined
by Aaron McBride.

15 / Luke meets Leia
for the last time.

"I felt really good about that scene. It was very emotional— for me and for Mark."

CARRIE FISHER

same with Harrison. And both times, their characters made comments about my hair! Which I encouraged, because otherwise, we'd say, 'Why didn't you call? What, you can't call through the Force? What are you using it for?' It was a fun scene to do, in the sense that we were really connected. It was so well written that you didn't have to act. There was complexity to the scene. Was Luke there? Was he not? Was he a ghost? Was he the Force? But he was real to me, and so we connected." ✪

1 /

CANTO BIGHT

WHERE LUXURY REIGNS

Galactic war didn't mean misery and suffering for everyone. Some saw the chaos it created as an opportunity for immense profit. Barons of industry and commerce who provided the First Order and Resistance with armories, ammunition, and technology increased their wealth beyond imagination. There were also criminals, waiting for the right opportunity to make a crooked deal.

FAR FROM THE CHAOS

There was no place like the resort city of Canto Bight on Cantonica—a haven for those who made fortunes contracting with both the First Order and the Resistance. Local law enforcement was in the pocket of Canto Bight's wealthy denizens,

constantly patrolling the streets, artificial coastline, and the Canto Casino and Racetrack. According to production designer Rick Heinrichs, Canto Bight proved to be the biggest challenge from the start of filming. "As we were steeping and immersing ourselves in the DNA of *Star Wars*, Canto Bight didn't quite fit any preconceived notions of anything

3 /

1 / Only the wealthiest can enter the famous Canto Casino and Racetrack.

2 / While war rages everywhere in the galaxy, life is luxurious on Cantonica.

3 / A wealthy guest of the famous Canto Casino and Racetrack. Art by creature concept designer and senior sculptor Ivan Manzella.

I had seen or come up against. I was confused about how to proceed. We looked at European cities, and we came across Dubrovnik, Croatia. First thing I thought was how clean it was, despite the fact it was old. It was a medieval town, and you would expect a place like that to be more of a ruin. The streets were impeccable and well taken care of, and there was a sense of history to the place. It was an environment that people would be familiar with. It was upon that idea that we expanded, adding *Star Wars* architectural elements to the existing look and feel of Dubrovnik."

A SPARKLING JEWEL
Canto Casino and Racetrack was the most exclusive place on Cantonica. Including luxurious restaurants, a deluxe hotel, a shopping concourse, game rooms, and a fathier racetrack, this was where the galaxy's elite spent their wealth, taking chances on games like Hazard Toss (the clientele's favorite dice game). Only politicians, celebrities, and business magnates could afford these expensive pleasures, but spies and master codebreakers could hide among them. "The casino was a joy for everybody to get involved with, particularly the creatures," said Chris Lowe, supervising art director. "The crew had a fantastic time making hundreds of creatures. We had to build this very large, cavernous gambling space with a bar in it that would take the action sequence [when the fathiers escape]. It ended up being so big that we split it across two stages. Not just for scale reasons, but for schedule reasons as well." To make everything work in this incredible set, communication between departments was essential. "The casino was an excellent example of how you integrate all the departments together," continued Lowe. "We had

4 / The stunning Canto Casino and Racetrack. Art by Roberto Fernández Castro and Rick Heinrichs.

5 / Canto Bight at night as imagined by concept artist Jaime Jones.

the stunt team pulling the gaming tables; we had creatures working, puppeteers underneath the tables; lighting effects; camera effects. There was a large wire camera in there. It was an amalgamation of every department."

SOMETHING MAGICAL

Finn and Rose planned to sneak aboard the enemy's flagship, the *Supremacy*, to disable the hyperspace tracker and save the Resistance fleet. But to make it work, they needed a codebreaker. The only place they could find one was the casino city Canto Bight, where the marvelous fathiers ran on a racetrack. "At Canto Bight, Rose and Finn stumbled into a stable where there are these creatures," recalled Kelly Marie Tran, who played Rose. "These beautiful, majestic animals! They were [Rose's sister] Paige's favorites. I saw them as unicorns, something that

Rose and Paige had dreamed about their whole lives. They had pictures on their walls of these animals. Rose finally sees them in real life, and she sees that these really rich war profiteers have the fathiers in cages. They're racing them, whipping them. The animals are so sad and trapped. In order to get away from the Canto Bight police, Rose and Finn team up with a stable boy and let all the fathiers loose. They trash the casino, and it's this awesome moment. I can't say enough about how amazing the creatures department was, and how much time went into creating these animals. The first time I acted opposite a fathier—let's be clear, it's a fake animal. Still, I cried! It was so beautiful and so sad. It took a lot of work to make something seem that real. I was so lucky to watch this process and see how much work went into everything. To see the end product was magical, to say the least."

6 / Every casino guest dreamed of making a fortune betting on the magnificent racing fathiers—four-legged, three-meter-high animals of unknown origin whose speed and power always delighted the wealthy spectators. Pictured here are 3D models created by Industrial Light & Magic.

7 / The fathiers race around the Canto Bight track in this concept art by Aaron McBride.

8 / Contessa Alissyndrex, the countess of Canto Bight who presided over the city, in this concept art by creature concept designer and senior sculptor Ivan Manzella.

11 /

DON'T JOIN

The thieves and pickpockets who ended up in the Canto Bight jail didn't plan on getting caught... all except for one. DJ let the local police arrest him on purpose. As he explained to his cellmates, jail was the only place where he could sleep without worrying about the authorities. "He was a cynic," explained actor Benicio del Toro, who played DJ. "He believed that good guys and bad guys are just basically the same. And he was a profiteer. He profited from the eternal war of good and evil. He was an opportunist, but could get you out of a jam, and get you in a jam." A self-proclaimed victim of societal inequity, DJ only cared about money. He would work indifferently for the Resistance or the First Order—his choice solely determined by how much he would make. That attitude perfectly reflected his only belief and his nickname: "Don't Join." When they infiltrated the *Supremacy*, DJ helped Finn, Rose, and BB-8 make their way to the hyperspace tracker, but they were caught before they could disable it. DJ would do anything he could to stay alive, and he did: he sold Finn and Rose out for his own freedom, revealing the Resistance evacuation plan on Crait. "He would work for the highest bidder," continued del Toro. "And he thought the First Order had more money than the Resistance, so you could imagine which side he picked. Basically, he's a mercenary." ☻

9 / DJ steals the luxury yacht Libertine and helps Rose and Finn escape, but he just does that for money.

10 / Director Rian Johnson and actor Benicio del Toro (DJ) "infiltrating" the *Supremacy* set.

11 / The unscrupulous and resourceful DJ. Art by Jock.

12 / If Rose is the angel on Finn's shoulder, DJ represents something quite the opposite, as Benicio del Toro said: "He was like this little devil on Finn's shoulder that was trying to make him see a different side or different approach to living in the galaxy."

12 /

THE SKYWALKER SAGA CONCLUDES

THE RISE OF SKYWALKER

THE RISE OF SKYWALKER
KYLO REN
DREAMING AN EMPIRE

The power of Supreme Leader Ren is threatened. Despite the unmatched fleet and army he inherited from his predecessor, systems and planets still rebel all across the galaxy. But there's something even worse. Kylo Ren has discovered that Snoke was nothing but a servant. Someone else is behind the First Order, a mysterious entity hiding in the shadows of Exegol, in the Unknown Regions.

AN UNEXPECTED DISCOVERY
The only way to find Exegol, and the secretive figure hiding there, was to use a wayfinder. The wayfinders were ancient lodestones that helped pilots find safe paths through navigationally challenging stretches of space back in the early days of hyperspace exploration. Only two pointed to Exegol; one belonged to Darth Vader, which was found on Mustafar. Once again, Kylo Ren's fate was tied to his grandfather's, but would it turn out to be the same? "When J.J. Abrams and I first met," says Adam Driver, "he told me to imagine a journey for Kylo that was opposite of Darth Vader. Whereas Vader was very confident when the audience first meets him, over the course of three movies he is chipped away

> ## "The journey Kylo went through really opened up my imagination as an actor."
> ADAM DRIVER

at until he was at his most vulnerable. Kylo's journey was almost the complete opposite. He started out very vulnerable, very childlike, and then over time he gained experience, became hardened and more assured about the choices he needed to make. The journey Kylo went through really opened up my imagination as an actor." After recovering the wayfinder Ren reached the ashy world of Exegol, where he made an unexpected discovery: a fleet that could bring a definitive end to the galactic rebellion, built by the Sith Eternal cultists. These loyal servants worked for a generation to keep the Sith tradition alive, waiting for the New Empire to rise.

3 /

4 /

1 / Kylo Ren wearing his reforged helmet. (See previous spread)

2 / Kylo Ren using his Force abilities to resist the *Millennium Falcon* thrusters and hold himself inside the hangar of his Star Destroyer. (See previous spread)

3 / Looking for the Sith wayfinder that can take him to Exegol, Supreme Leader Ren slays the barbarians protecting Darth Vader's castle on the volcanic planet Mustafar. Art by concept artist Andrée Wallin.

4 / Ren and Rey meet on the planet Kijimi, but they are not in the same place: Rey is aboard Ren's flagship above the planet, and Ren is in the streets of Kijimi City. Their Force connection lets them see each other.

THE DYAD

To claim the immense Exegol fleet, to sit on the Emperor's throne, Kylo Ren had to find Rey and turn her to the dark side. For they were the dyad of the legend, twins of the Force, a pairing that had not been seen for generations. Not only did they share a bond that connected them through any distance, but they also share an unimaginable power. If Rey became a Jedi, the First Order would fall and Ren would die. With this awareness, sensed through the Force, the Supreme Leader reconnected with Luke Skywalker's

apprentice. Ren couldn't read Rey's mind or find out where she was or where she was headed, but he could feel her emotions and could tell there was conflict in her. Persuading Rey to surrender to the dark side, to what she is destined to become, didn't seem impossible to him. As producer Kathleen Kennedy explains, this relationship is the core of the film: "It really drove the story in this particular saga, and I thought it was hugely emotional. It was interesting to watch Daisy and Adam delve into exactly what their characters' relationships meant to the two of them."

BACK TO THE KNIGHTS

Finding Rey was Kylo Ren's priority. Aware that he couldn't rely only on General Hux and his First Order stormtroopers, the Supreme Leader rejoined the Knights of Ren—the powerful followers gifted to him by Snoke. These Force-sensitive hunters, equipped with technologically modified primitive weapons and heavily customized blasters, only obeyed his orders. Trudgen was the collector. He wielded a gigantic vibrocleaver—featuring ultrasonic vibro-technology that made it extremely sharp—and wore part of a death trooper's mask he most likely took from a defeated adversary. Kuruk was the rifleman and the pilot of the group's customized ship, the *Night Buzzard*. With his multi-barreled custom-designed rifle, Kuruk usually covered the other Knights from a distant point during assaults. Ap'Lek was the strategist. He used his skills to lure opponents into a trap. A master of deception, Ap'Lek came into possession of a Mandalorian executioner's ax. Ushar was in charge of the prisoners. Cruel and merciless, he only respected those who fought back, reserving torture and punishment for those who begged for their lives. His weapon was a war club, equipped with a concussion field generator. Cardo was the armorer. An expert in cannons and flamethrowers, he preferred to take down any enemy with heavy firepower. Finally, there's Vicrul. Guided by his dark side abilities— extraordinary reflexes and the power to instill fear in his prey—Vicrul loved to strike his victims closely, using an ultrasonic-enhanced scythe.

5 /

6 /

5 / The Knights of Ren render compilation. Art by costume modeller Sam Williams.

6 / For centuries the Unknown Regions had heard terrible stories about the Knights of Ren, the dark warriors who pillaged the unmapped territories. Unfortunately for the rest of the galaxy, the legend became a reality.

7 /

8 /

Hux is now considered to be an unreliable officer.

7 / Even though he was not held in the same regard as before, General Hux did not abandon his scheming nature, as Domhnall Gleeson says: "You very much get the impression he has given everything, outside of his actual life, over to being number one. Anything less than that would be disappointing."

8 / Honoring his dark side training, Kylo Ren recovered the fragments of his shattered helmet from the *Supremacy* and took them to a Sith alchemist, who put them together using ancient techniques. In this on-set photo, the mask shows the red alchemical lattice of Sarrassian iron used to reforge it.

RECRUITS AND VETERANS

To expand its reach, and keep rebelling systems under control, Ren's First Order had extended its recruiting program and increased the raids in every occupied territory. Young children were taken from their homes, educated, and trained to become stormtroopers or pilots. Equipped with advanced weapons, armors, and backpack units, they helped pacify cities and occupy planets under the direction of the Supreme Council—the new First Order high command created by the Supreme Leader. Aboard his flagship, the *Steadfast*, Kylo Ren exercises his authority over everyone, especially General Hux. Once the key man in the First Order military strategy, Hux was now considered to be an unreliable officer. "As you see the First Order, it was very clear Hux was not vying anymore for supremacy with Kylo," says actor Domhnall Gleeson, who plays Hux. "Before, they could both run to dad, to Snoke, and rat the other one out. All that was gone and Ren was in charge, to the point where Kylo wasn't even concerned with Hux anymore—Ren just kept him there because it was easier than losing him." Armitage Hux now served under Allegiant General Pryde, a survivor of the Battle of Jakku that followed the destruction of the second Death Star thirty years prior. In charge of both ground and space-based forces, Pryde was efficient but also ambitious. He considered the Sith fleet waiting on Exegol an indispensable asset to build the future of the First Order. ✦

9 /

9 / Kylo Ren in his sanctuary private rooms aboard the *Steadfast*. Behind him is Darth Vader's mangled helmet. Art by Andrée Wallin.

10 / Allegiant General Pryde hid in the Unknown Regions after the dismantling of the Galactic Empire. He reemerged when Snoke gave him the command of the *Steadfast* Star Destroyer.

REY

HEART OF THE RESISTANCE

2 /

O nce just a scavenger, Rey from Jakku had become a spark that gave hope to the Resistance. Surrounded by the warmth of her new friends, guided by General Leia, Rey trained on Ajan Kloss, where the rebel forces took refuge after the Battle of Crait. But obscured visions of distant planets and a dark future followed the young Jedi. The Force was trying to tell her something.

BECOMING A JEDI

On Ajan Kloss, the verdant planet in the Outer Rim that became the new home of the Resistance, Rey challenged her abilities. She ran through the rainforests, practiced with Luke's lightsaber, which she had repaired after it was split apart aboard the *Supremacy*, and deflected blasts from training remotes. This was how Leia herself trained thirty years prior with the help of her brother, Luke—before she abandoned the Jedi path and decided her future lay elsewhere. "Working on the previous movies was really exhausting," said actress Daisy Ridley, who plays Rey. "This time I wanted to be sure I had

"When it came time to do all the required stunts, I felt I was ready for the challenge."

DAISY RIDLEY

enough stamina; I wanted to be healthy and, most importantly, ready. I even started kickboxing. When it came time to do all the required stunts, I felt I was ready for the challenge. Mentally, I had to prepare to do some rather terrifying things, and I had to completely trust the stunt team I was working with. I was doing things I never thought I would be doing, such as being strapped into a harness connected to wires and diving off a thirty-foot-tall platform. But because I trusted the team around me, I felt I could do anything they asked me to."

1 / Rey in the Pasaana desert. The planet reminds her of Jakku, even though among its people, she finds a kindness she has never experienced before. (See previous spread)

2 / Rey training with the Marksman-H combat remotes. The red one is the most aggressive of all, its blasts offering a significant challenge. (See previous spread)

3 / Rey holding the ignited lightsaber once owned by Anakin Skywalker and then passed on to his son, Luke, through Obi-Wan Kenobi.

4 / Rey receives a lightsaber from Leia. Aware her days are numbered, General Organa is concerned about Rey's visions. The only way to prevent the young Jedi from joining the dark side is by having faith in her and telling her not to ever be afraid of who she is. Art by concept artists Andrée Wallin and Adam Baines.

IN NEED OF ANSWERS

Even though she considers Leia a master, Rey couldn't tell her the truth about her visions, in which she is the new Dark Lord of the Sith. The young Jedi doesn't know if joining the dark side is in her destiny, but she was afraid it was inevitable. In need of guidance, full of questions, Rey searched the Jedi texts she took from Luke Skywalker's library on Ahch-To. Written by masters and apprentices across the centuries, these books couldn't help her make sense of those visions, but it's among their pages that Rey found the name Exegol, just when Finn and Poe came back from a secret mission with vital information. On the world of Exegol, in the Unknown Regions, followers of the Sith had been building a fleet of thousands of Star Destroyers for ages. As he wrote in the Jedi texts, Luke was also looking for Exegol, and his trail took him to the planet Pasaana. In a mysterious way, the Jedi scriptures were bringing Rey closer to the truth. The last part of the journey started for Rey, for the actress

"Rey emerged as a powerful figure in these stories."

KATHLEEN KENNEDY

who played her, and for the audience. As producer Kathleen Kennedy says: "It was fascinating to watch Daisy get into a role like Rey at nineteen or twenty years old and then to watch her mature in the role into her mid-20s. When she first began, nobody knew who she was, she was just getting started in the business. Even the idea of getting strong physically, and being able to handle the stunts and the saber fights and things like that, was all new to her. However, she emerged as a powerful figure in these stories. I thought there was an interesting parallel to Daisy and Rey's development that really came through in the movie."

5 /

6 /

5 /
5 / Rey's vision showed the young Jedi a version of herself who came from the dark side of the Force.

6 / R2-D2 and C-3PO near an A-wing starfighter on Ajan Kloss. Anthony Daniels is the only actor to appear in every *Star Wars* movie. "On my final day of shooting," he said, "it was very moving, a very bittersweet moment. Making these movies has been hard work, but it has also been fun and a great joy for me. I have been in *Star Wars* since day one out in Tunisia in 1976, so it was quite something to have survived this long. It was quite a ride."

7 / As Daisy Ridley clarifies, her look didn't differ too much from the previous films: "My costume was pretty much white, which was great because we were filming in the sun. As for the hair, the team went for something that looked slightly different than before, but still retained the same silhouette. My makeup pretty much stayed the same—all natural." Art by Glyn Dillon.

7 /

THE FUTURE OF THE GALAXY

The Resistance survived the Battle of Crait. Since then, new allies joined General Leia's rebel movement. Their number was still not enough to overcome the First Order, though, and the fleet they could count on was at its lowest point. Despite months of scrounging for new ships all over the galaxy, it only consisted of a squadron of starfighters: a few A-wings, B-wings, Y-wings, and the signature vessel of the Rebel Alliance, X-wings. "At this point, the Resistance had been decimated, and there was only a small group left," explains actor Oscar Isaac, who played Poe Dameron. "Some time has passed since the events of *The Last Jedi*, which enabled the group to get some help, gather a few allies, and recruit some new Resistance fighters. However, despite this, they were still scrambling to find even more help somewhere in the galaxy. Poe and Finn had been on some rather insane missions desperately trying to find a way to fight back against the First Order."

8 /

8 / Finn at the Resistance base on Ajan Kloss. As John Boyega recalls: "Costume designer Michael Kaplan did a great job. This time around, Finn has his own thing going, you know? A new style. He basically went to the Resistance beauty camp. He's now color-coordinating: blue and brown pants, brown waistcoat. He has new hair. I mean, in the stress of war, why not look good fighting?"

9 / An expert in ancient history and Sith lore, Beaumont Kin is one of the most important members of the Resistance's intelligence division.

10 /Chewbacca, Finn, and Poe aboard the *Millennium Falcon* during the mission in which they receive a secret message coming from a spy in the First Order: a massive Sith fleet is stationed in the Unknown Regions.

11 / Poe, Rose Tico, and Finn on Ajan Kloss. Rose is now a military commander: she developed new systems that could help the Resistance against the extremely advanced First Order science.

FRIENDS AND FIGHTERS

After numerous daring missions for the Resistance, former stormtrooper FN-2187 had changed. Embracing General Organa's cause, Finn was aware of the importance of his role: defeating the First Order meant no more kids would be taken from their planets and turned into obedient soldiers. "I definitely wanted Finn to eventually find his place," says actor John Boyega, "to be part of a team he's not only fighting for, but rooting for as well. I wanted Finn to become strong and not have his strength always questioned. I wanted to show his growth and to show he has an understanding of his world and the people around him, as well as his past."

On a similar path is Poe Dameron. Skilled pilot and expert field agent, Poe had to prove he was the leader the Resistance needed, something he had to achieve with the help of his friends, especially Finn. The friendship between the two characters goes beyond the narrative as Isaac explains: "As much as these movies are about the Skywalker saga, for me doing them has also been the saga of meeting John Boyega and to experience this adventure with him. He has such a beautiful heart and is such a beautiful person. I definitely admire him. My first screen test back on *The Force Awakens* was with John, in the TIE fighter. And we've been back to back ever since. The exciting thing about *The Rise of Skywalker* is John and I got a chance to really work together, to interact with one another and have fun. And the reason it was so fun to work on this movie is that he and I got to do so much together. I just love him."

> "I wanted Finn to become strong."
> JOHN BOYEGA

9 /

10 /

11 /

12 /

12 / Rey takes back her place aboard the *Millennium Falcon* with Chewbacca, Poe Dameron, and Finn. Her relationship with them, especially the latter two, is one of the distinctive traits of the film as Oscar Isaac says: "J.J. put the trio together, and I think it definitely helped capture some of the spirit from the original trilogy. There was a dynamic between the three characters that was great."

13 / Resistance technicians working on the *Tantive IV* on Ajan Kloss. This is the ship Princess Leia used to escape the Battle of Scarif with the stolen Death Star plans before the Battle of Yavin. Art by ILM concept artist Michael Sheffels.

13 /

ACROSS THE GALAXY

UNRAVELING THE MYSTERY

The way to Exegol is from Pasaana, a desert planet in the Ombakand sector, in the Expansion Region. Pasaana was where Luke Skywalker had to give up his quest for Exegol, and where Rey and her friends picked it up. This was only the first planet they visited: from Pasaana, through the lawless and cold Kijimi, they got to Kef Bir before finding an unexpected route to Exegol.

RENDEZVOUS ON PASAANA

As he himself wrote in the Jedi texts, Luke Skywalker needed the Emperor's wayfinder to locate Exegol. Together with an old ally, the Jedi Master learned that a hunter of Sith relics, Ochi of Bestoon, knew where the ancient artifact was. The two followed Ochi to Pasaana, but the hunter vanished in the desert, leaving his empty

ship behind. The investigation ended, and Luke left the planet. But his ally didn't. When Rey, Finn, Poe, BB-8, Chewbacca, and C-3PO arrived on Pasaana, aboard the *Millennium Falcon*, they found themselves in the middle of a local festival. Among the thousands of visitors, they were identified by a stormtrooper, and Luke's ally appeared to save them, revealing his identity: he was Lando Calrissian, the hero who helped the Rebel Alliance destroy the Empire. After the New Republic was elected, Lando started a family, but the First Order took his daughter and turned her into a stormtrooper. Lando looked for her to no avail. Six years later, he helped his old friend Skywalker in his research on Exegol, and when Luke left Pasaana empty-handed, Lando decided to stay, hoping the desert would help him forget what happened. "At times

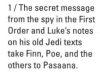

2 / Aboard his beloved *Millennium Falcon,* Lando has the chance to repeat history and help Leia free the galaxy from the returning Sith.

3

I wondered if Lando would return. So I was very happy about being asked to come back," says Billy Dee Williams, who played Lando in the original trilogy. About working with Williams, Daisy Ridley says: "Billy Dee, who's such a suave, suave man, brought so much joy to the set. It was great he came back, and in this movie. There was a particular scene where the rest of us were so exhausted, yet he just kept going! He didn't need any rest or anything. And his overall vibe was just great."

"I was very happy about being asked to come back."

BILLY DEE WILLIAMS

3 / Kylo Ren arrives on Pasaana aboard his TIE whisper. Rey runs from it to unexpectedly jump when it's close and cut through its armored cockpit with her lightsaber.
Art by ILM London senior art director Stephen Tappin.

4 /

4 / In the tunnels under Pasaana, the rebels meet an armored snake, otherwise known as a vexis. Art by concept artist Adam Brockbank.

"Zorii is very much a survivor."

KERI RUSSELL

A BLADE HIDDEN IN THE DESERT

Chased by a First Order unit of stormtroopers and jet troopers—who could fly thanks to their integrated jet packs—Rey and the others managed to escape aboard two stolen skimmers. Once they got rid of the pursuers, the Resistance fighters found Ochi's abandoned ship, but before they can enter the derelict spacecraft, they disappeared into the Shifting Mires. Similar to quicksand, the Shifting Mires took them below the dunes of Pasaana to a network of tunnels. It's inside one of those tunnels that they found the remains of Ochi of Bestoon. From his belt, Rey retrieved an ornate knife, etched with runic symbols. C-3PO explained that those symbols revealed the location to the Emperor's wayfinder. Unfortunately, the droid's Republic programming forbade him from translating or sharing any Sith knowledge. Meanwhile, the First Order confiscated the *Millennium Falcon*, forcing the rebels, once they exited the tunnels, to leave Pasaana aboard Ochi's ship. There, behind some crates covered in dust and cobwebs, BB-8 found Ochi's old droid, a little wheeled unit named D-O.

AMONG THE KIJIMI THIEVES

The only way to make C-3PO translate the forbidden language of the Sith was to bypass his programming, a dangerous practice only a criminal droidsmith could perform. Poe Dameron happened to know one: Babu Frik, who lived on the cold and dangerous world Kijimi. Far away from justice and law, but not from the First Order that keeps taking its children to turn them into stormtroopers, Kijimi had been where criminals settled since the collapse of the Empire. Poe himself spent five years as a member of the local spice runners gang when he was younger, a secret he kept from his friends until they arrived on the planet. The truth was revealed by a gunslinger called Zorii Bliss, the leader of the spice runners, who caught the rebels off guard. Putting old grudges behind—she initially wanted to shoot Poe with her blasters—Zorii decided to take her former mate and his friends to Babu Frik. "She kind of lives in the gray area between the light and the dark," says actress Keri Russell about her character. "She's done some rather sketchy things in her lifetime and she has a tough exterior—she's very much a survivor." Once the group reached Babu Frik's workshop in the Thieves' Quarter of Kijimi City, the legendary droidsmith warned them: bypassing the security measures that protect C-3PO's programming could cause a complete loss of memory. It was a difficult choice only C-3PO could make, but the droid well knew what was at stake and accepts.

6 /

5 / Rey, Poe, and Finn look for a droidsmith in the Thieves' Quarter of Kijimi City. Art by concept artist Jon McCoy.

6 / Sophisticated and equipped with sensors, a powerful comlink, and life-support systems, Zorii's bronzium helmet also hides her features. "The costume is the coolest one I've ever worn!" says actress Keri Russell. "It has this cool helmet that I really loved, because there was such a power to wearing it. There's something in being hidden that innately gives you this other kind of strength. It's very unnerving to people when they can't see you, but you can see them."

7 / Found on Kijimi, Babu Frik is nine inches tall, the perfect size for a droidsmith.

8 /

A DEATH STAR ON KEF BIR

C-3PO had forgotten everything about his past life, including his participation in the Galactic Civil War alongside his best friend, R2-D2. But after the procedure, he could reveal the location of the Emperor's wayfinder: Kef Bir, the ocean moon of Endor, where a massive fragment of the second Death Star crashed after the Imperial battle station was destroyed by the Rebel Alliance. The fragment contained the Emperor's throne room and the Imperial vault, where the wayfinder was sealed. Kef Bir should be uninhabited, but after the *Falcon* landed, its crew met a band of orbak riders led by a

woman. Her name was Jannah. Like Finn, Jannah and her companions were all stormtroopers, members of Company 77. When their superiors ordered them to fire on civilians, they all mutinied after having the same feeling, which Finn believed originated in the Force. As a nomadic tribe, they roamed the islands of Kef Bir atop their tamed orbaks. "An orbak is a four-legged creature and very furry," explained actress Naomi Ackie, who played Jannah. "To prepare for the role meant months of training on horseback, which I became very adept at. Afterward, I could ride using one hand, no hands, and shoot a bow and arrow while doing it! When I started the journey, I was terrified of

9 /

8 / C-3PO's photoreceptors become red when he interprets the forbidden Sith language after Babu Frik has bypassed his programming.

9 / Lightsaber duel aboard the ruins of the second Death Star. Art by Andrée Wallin and Stephen Tappin.

10 / Finn and Jannah try to reach Rey during her duel with Kylo Ren, but they can't: using their Force abilities, the two opponents have jumped too far.

11 / Most of Jannah's equipment has been salvaged from the Death Star wreckage. Art by chief costume concept artist Glyn Dillon.

10 /

horses as I had never seen one up close. I'm from East London, and there aren't any horses around there." Jannah used a powered bow she built herself from blaster rifles. "It's not only awesome, but deadly," continues Ackie. "It's a two-handed weapon that she could swing from one side to the other. She's a very resourceful person, by the way. She actually made her own arrows out of old material and whatever else she could find in her environment."

Like Finn, Jannah and her companions were once stormtroopers.

11 /

The fate of the entire Resistance is in the young Jedi's hands.

FACING THE DARK SIDE

Titanic waves surrounded the ruins of the Death Star. Rey sailed across the violent ocean from the cliffs of Dead Empire, as Company 77 called the coast, using a sea skiff—a modified vehicle built with fragments from the Imperial superweapon, as well as Alliance starfighters that fell on the moon with it. Rey couldn't wait for the tide to fall as Jannah suggested; she had to retrieve the Emperor's wayfinder and locate Exegol before the Sith fleet leaves the Unknown Regions. Once she reached the Death Star ruins and entered the throne room, Rey felt the power of the dark side, once again suffering visions of a terrifying future. Then Kylo Ren arrived, and the two engaged in a fiery duel. Finn and Jannah, who followed Rey with a second sea skiff, couldn't intervene. The fate of the entire Resistance was in the young Jedi's hands. As Daisy Ridley explains, the lightsaber fight with Adam Driver (Kylo Ren) was one of the most challenging scenes for her to shoot. "What made it more challenging than the other lightsaber fights was that we were being doused with water cannons the whole time. And since it was November in England, it was very cold as well. As far as just being the most challenging scene, that would have to have been working atop the speeders while filming in Jordan [during the Pasaana chase sequence]. The vehicle we were riding on was tilted a certain way, which really made my knees hurt by the end of the day. And because we had wind machines constantly going, a piece of sand scratched my eye, causing it to become puffy and irritated. It's weird because technically we didn't really look like we were doing anything. But the way the vehicle moved, and because of the many hours we were on it, made it tough." ☯

12 / In the same room where Luke redeemed his father, Rey is ready to cross lightsabers with Darth Vader's grandson.

13 / Rey and Kylo fighting in the middle of Kef Bir's raging oceans. "The battle was really physically exhausting," says Daisy Ridley, "but at the same time very exciting. I mean, we were wet and soaked and cold and on wires. I loved it."

14 / The incredible Force-jumps during Rey and Kylo's duel aboard the ruins of the second Death Star. Art by co-production designer Kevin Jenkins.

1 /

ON EXEGOL

THE RETURN OF THE SITH

An army comprising of thousands of starfighters, hundreds of warships, an endless number of stormtroopers, officers, engineers, and pilots. This was the Final Order, the fearsome Sith fleet that waited in underground launch bays beneath the surface of Exegol. If it were ever to leave the planet, it couldn't be stopped, resulting in the creation of a formidable New Empire. The Resistance had to strike immediately, when the fleet was at its most vulnerable.

> "It's not just the end of three movies, but rather the end of nine movies."
>
> J.J. ABRAMS

1 / The Final Order rising from the surface of Exegol.

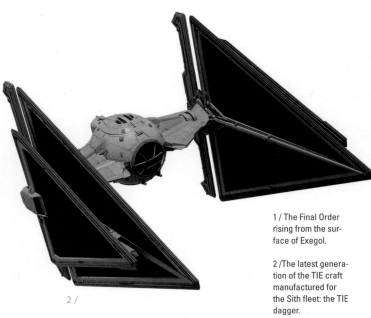

2 /

2 / The latest generation of the TIE craft manufactured for the Sith fleet: the TIE dagger.

THE FINAL MENACE

The Resistance did not have enough ships, and certainly not enough fighters, to oppose the Final Order. But as Poe Dameron and his friends knew, they had to find a way, any way, to prevent the Sith Order from resurrecting or the galaxy would be subdued to the dark side of the Force. The power of the fleet built in decades by the Sith engineers was unbelievable: the *Xyston*-class Star Destroyers, based on the classic *Imperial*-class design, were equipped with a planet-killing axial superlaser that rivaled the one the Death Star was armed with. One of these warships alone could destroy an entire planet. Supporting these flying fortresses were the new TIE daggers, perfected with triangular solar panels, that efficiently spread deflector-shield energy and keep the fighters' power cells energized. But that was not all. To ensure the control of every system, the Sith Eternal cultists created the Sith stormtroopers, their own version of the Imperial and First Order stormtroopers. Equipped with a quadru-ple-layered gammaplast armor, high-tech helmets that

could calculate the outcomes of different tactics in a short time, and heavy ST-W-48 rifles with quarrel-bolt launchers, these dark soldiers were organized in legions, amounting to five thousand units. More devoted and efficient than their First Order predecessors, thanks to their flash imprinting and loyal conditioning, they would never mutiny. The battle against this army not only represented the end of the war against the First Order but the end of an entire saga, as director J.J. Abrams says: "As a filmmaker, to bring the movie to a conclusion that it and the fans deserve—and it's not just the end of three movies, but rather the end of nine movies—there was certainly a lot to consider. Working with Chris Terrio, who wrote the script with me, we never wanted to forget what made *Star Wars* potent and resonant and alive." ☙

3 / A Sith fleet officer. Art by Glyn Dillon.

4 / The helmet of a Sith trooper. Art by Glyn Dillon.

5 / Equipped with NJP-900 packs, the Sith jet troopers are the ultimate elite assault force.

6 / The red uniform of the Sith troopers is reminiscent of the Sith lightsaber blades, as well as of the Emperor's elite guards.

7 / Sith royal guards. Art by prop concept designer Matt Savage.

8 / A Sith trooper with the supplied SONN-BLAS FWMB 10B repeating blaster. Art by Glyn Dillon.

6 /

STAR WARS LIBRARY

STAR WARS: THE EMPIRE STRIKES BACK: THE OFFICIAL COLLECTOR'S EDITION

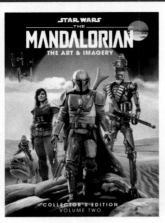

THE MANDALORIAN THE ART AND IMAGERY VOLUME 2

STAR WARS: THE RISE OF SKYWALKER: THE OFFICIAL COLLECTOR'S EDITION

STAR WARS: THE SKYWALKER SAGA THE OFFICIAL MOVIE COMPANION

- *ROGUE ONE: A STAR WARS STORY* THE OFFICIAL COLLECTOR'S EDITION
- *ROGUE ONE: A STAR WARS STORY* THE OFFICIAL MISSION DEBRIEF
- *STAR WARS: THE LAST JEDI* THE OFFICIAL COLLECTOR'S EDITION
- *STAR WARS: THE LAST JEDI* THE OFFICIAL MOVIE COMPANION
- *STAR WARS: THE LAST JEDI* THE ULTIMATE GUIDE
- *SOLO: A STAR WARS STORY*

- THE OFFICIAL COLLECTOR'S EDITION
- *SOLO: A STAR WARS STORY* THE ULTIMATE GUIDE
- **THE BEST OF** *STAR WARS INSIDER* VOLUME 1
- **THE BEST OF** *STAR WARS INSIDER* VOLUME 2
- **THE BEST OF** *STAR WARS INSIDER* VOLUME 3
- **THE BEST OF** *STAR WARS INSIDER* VOLUME 4

- *STAR WARS:* LORDS OF THE SITH
- *STAR WARS:* HEROES OF THE FORCE
- *STAR WARS:* ICONS OF THE GALAXY
- *STAR WARS:* THE SAGA BEGINS
- *STAR WARS* THE ORIGINAL TRILOGY
- *STAR WARS:* ROGUES, SCOUNDRELS AND BOUNTY HUNTERS
- *STAR WARS* CREATURES, ALIENS, AND DROIDS
- *STAR WARS: THE RISE OF SKYWALKER* THE OFFICIAL COLLECTOR'S EDITION

- *THE MANDALORIAN* THE ART AND IMAGERY VOLUME 1
- *THE MANDALORIAN* THE ART AND IMAGERY VOLUME 2
- *STAR WARS: THE EMPIRE STRIKES BACK* THE 40TH ANNIVERSARY COLLCTORS' EDITION
- *STAR WARS: AGE OF RESISTANCE* THE OFFICIAL COLLCTORS' EDITION
- *STAR WARS: THE SKYWALKER SAGA* THE OFFICIAL COLLECTOR'S EDITION

MARVEL LIBRARY

THE X-MEN AND THE AVENGERS GAMMA QUEST OMNIBUS

MARVEL STUDIOS' THE COMPLETE AVENGERS

MARVEL STUDIOS' BLACK WIDOW

MARVEL: THE FIRST 80 YEARS

MARVEL CLASSIC NOVELS
- **SPIDER-MAN** THE VENOM FACTOR OMNIBUS
- **X-MEN AND THE AVENGERS** GAMMA QUEST OMNIBUS
- **X-MEN** MUTANT FACTOR OMNIBUS

NOVELS
- **ANT-MAN** NATURAL ENEMY
- **AVENGERS** EVERYBODY WANTS TO RULE THE WORLD
- **AVENGERS** INFINITY
- **BLACK PANTHER** WHO IS THE BLACK PANTHER?
- **CAPTAIN AMERICA** DARK DESIGNS

- **CAPTAIN MARVEL** LIBERATION RUN
- **CIVIL WAR**
- **DEADPOOL** PAWS
- **SPIDER-MAN** FOREVER YOUNG
- **SPIDER-MAN** KRAVEN'S LAST HUNT
- **THANOS** DEATH SENTENCE
- **VENOM** LETHAL PROTECTOR
- **X-MEN** DAYS OF FUTURE PAST
- **X-MEN** THE DARK PHOENIX SAGA
- **SPIDER-MAN** HOSTILE TAKEOVER

ARTBOOKS
- **MARVEL'S** *SPIDER-MAN* THE ART OF THE GAME
- **MARVEL** *CONTEST OF CHAMPIONS* THE ART OF THE BATTLEREALM
- *SPIDER-MAN: INTO THE SPIDERVERSE*
- **THE ART OF IRON MAN** 10TH ANNIVERSARY EDITION

MOVIE SPECIALS
- **MARVEL STUDIOS'** *ANT MAN & THE WASP*
- **MARVEL STUDIOS'** *AVENGERS: ENDGAME*

- **MARVEL STUDIOS'** *AVENGERS: INFINITY WAR*
- **MARVEL STUDIOS'** *BLACK PANTHER (COMPANION)*
- **MARVEL STUDIOS'** *BLACK WIDOW (SPECIAL)*
- **MARVEL STUDIOS'** *CAPTAIN MARVEL*
- **MARVEL STUDIOS'** *SPIDER-MAN: FAR FROM HOME*
- **MARVEL STUDIOS:** THE FIRST TEN YEARS
- **MARVEL STUDIOS'** *THOR: RAGNAROK*

- *SPIDER-MAN: INTO THE SPIDERVERSE*